The Wisdom of
Negative
Thinking

TONY HUMPHREYS, Ph.D.

THE CROSSING PRESS
FREEDOM, CALIFORNIA

First published in 1996 by Gill & MacMillan, Ltd., U.K.

For information on bulk purchases or group discounts for this and other
Crossing Press titles, please contact our Special Sales Manager at 800/777-1048.
Visit our Web site: **www.crossingpress.com**

Library of Congress Cataloging-in-Publication Data
Humphreys, Tony.
  The wisdom of negative thinking / Tony Humphreys.
    p. cm.
  Rev. ed. of: The power of 'negative' thinking.
  ISBN 1-58091-097-1 (pbk.)
    1. Negativism.   I. Humphreys, Tony. Power of 'negative' thinking.
  II. Title.
  BF698.35.N44 H85 2001
  158--dc21
                            2001032533

Dedicated To

Professor Peter Dempsey, friend and mentor
for the encouragement and safety
for exploration he provided

I wish to thank most warmly all the courageous clients whose openness propelled me into searching for more ways of understanding and healing myself and helping others to heal their wounded selves.

I want also to express my love and gratitude to my partner Helen Ruddle whose love, support, patience and editing of my ideas made the writing of this book emotionally safe and challenging.

CONTENTS

CHAPTER 1

PROTECTING YOURSELF IN AN UNSAFE WORLD

THE WORLD IS OFTEN NOT A SAFE PLACE TO BE

We live in a world of locks and bolts, guns, alarm systems, 'Neighbourhood Watch' systems, policing and insurance schemes to guard against all sorts of threats to our physical safety. It is no longer safe to walk alone on lonely country roads, remote forest paths or busy city streets. We are also aware of the risks to property. We are very alert to these threats to our physical safety and property, and we see the necessity and the creativity of developing behaviours and systems to protect ourselves. But what we are not so aware of are the multiple threats that exist to our emotional and social well-being. These emotional perils that children and adults face every day are, in many ways, an even greater threat to well-being than physical perils. Why? Because the prime need of people in our culture is to be loved, recognised, valued and accepted. Any threat to that emotional and social need poses great danger for people and so it is not surprising that, just as for physical threats, creative protections are developed to reduce or eliminate risks to emotional and social well-being. Where do these threats arise and what is their nature? They arise mainly in the following social systems:

- □ homes
- □ schools and classrooms

- communities
- workplaces.

The ways that an unsafe emotional atmosphere can develop in each of these systems are illustrated below.

Unsafe homes

The parental home is the first and most influential social system in our lives, while the second is the couple relationship. Most of us have been born into a family. As adults many of us are involved in a primary couple relationship. It is the nature of the relationships within these two systems that determines the level and intensity of the unsafety that can be experienced. Each family and couple relationship has its own unique culture and to truly understand a person's present-day insecurity as an adult you need a detailed biographical history of that person.

Threats to the emotional well-being of family members or to partners in a couple relationship are posed by interactions that are of either a conditional or a totally neglectful nature.

FEATURES OF CONDITIONAL INTERACTIONS

Withdrawal of love	Violence
Domination	Judgments
Control	Irritability
Aggression	Impatience
Passivity	Non-listening
Ridicule	Dismissiveness
Scoldings	Conformity
Hostile criticism	Overinvolvement

In conditional interactions the unsafety that is created is due to the sad fact that you do not feel loved for yourself, and the only way you can gain love is by meeting certain conditions. What uncertainty this creates! There never can be a guarantee that you will be able to measure up and meet these conditions. Typical conditions for gaining love and recognition in families and couple relationships are: be good, be perfect, be clever, be beautiful, be like me, be the same, be kind, be the helper, be quiet. Unsafety arises with these expectations because love is withdrawn in the form of the kind of punishing behaviours listed above if you do not toe the line. When people – whether children or adults – experience these punishing reactions, their emotional world becomes very unsafe and they are forced into ways of protecting themselves from further hurt. In much the same way as they would protect their physical lives by any means, people learn ways of defending themselves against these emotional perils. Much of this book is devoted to illustrating the very many creative strategies that human beings adopt to protect themselves in the face of emotional perils.

FEATURES OF TOTALLY NEGLECTFUL INTERACTIONS

- ☐ No demonstrations of love
- ☐ Physical abuse
- ☐ Sexual abuse
- ☐ Verbal abuse
- ☐ Neglect of physical welfare
- ☐ Emotionless reactions
- ☐ Hostile silences
- ☐ Lack of interest in each other's lives
- ☐ Depression
- ☐ Hopelessness
- ☐ Apathy
- ☐ Extreme hostility
- ☐ Lack of involvement with each other
- ☐ Extreme withdrawal
- ☐ Alcoholism
- ☐ Drug addiction

The level of emotional unsafety in homes where relationships are characterised by conditionality is always threatening, but is not as devastating as in homes where relationships are of a totally neglectful nature. This is so because conditionality provides some possibilities for gaining love and recognition, whereas total neglect provides no such possibilities.

It does not take much imagination to envisage the depth and intensity of unsafety that is created within homes characterised by total neglect. The protections needed in such an unsafe environment have to match the extremes of the neglectful behaviours experienced.

Unsafe schools and classrooms

The third most powerful social system of which we become members in the course of our lives is the school. There are many people who still rage at the humiliation they experienced during their time in school. I have made a deliberate distinction between schools and classrooms. We all have had teachers who were kind, understanding, caring and concerned, and others who were hostile, critical, violent, cynical and sarcastic. Clearly the emotional dangers experienced in the classrooms of the latter were great indeed.

The school itself also tends to have its own unique atmosphere. In the school that promotes an ethos of respect and valuing of all its members, you can sense intuitively the safety of the atmosphere. In schools where no such ethos has been developed, interactions that are of a threatening nature to students and teachers may go unnoticed and are certainly not confronted. Bullying, hostile teasing, stealing, drug trafficking, apathy and uncaring behaviour are some of the features of these schools. Students and teachers do not feel safe coming into this environment and all sorts of protective behaviours necessarily evolve: playing truant, absenteeism, aggression and withdrawal. Unsafety in schools and classrooms creates a variety of fears:

- □ Fear of failure
- □ Fear of criticism
- □ Fear of humiliation
- □ Fear of ridicule
- □ Fear of scolding
- □ Fear of not being good enough
- □ Fear of appearing 'foolish' and 'stupid'
- □ Fear of showing weaknesses
- □ Fear of cynicism and sarcasm
- □ Fear of bullying
- □ Fear of being compared to others
- □ Fear of being teased
- □ Fear of being ostracised
- □ Fear of not being accepted and valued

It is no wonder that both students and teachers have to take refuge in behaviours that creatively protect them from the realisation of these fears. The nature and breadth of these necessary protective internal and external actions will emerge as you read this book.

Unsafe communities

We live in neighbourhoods of one kind or another. I live in a rural area not far from a village of two pubs, a shop, a church, a scattering of houses and a community hall. Generally speaking it is a safe place to be, although in the recent past there were some robberies with violence in the area which led to more cautiousness among people. What I like about my neighbourhood is that people seem to respect and value differences between one another and there is no strong push towards conformity, not even towards religious conformity, although the latter has been a strong feature of local community life. There is also a friendliness between people. As in all communities, you have the 'rogue', the 'sharp operator' and the overinquisitive person, but you learn, sometimes after some personal cost, to guard against the exploitative behaviours of these people.

There are communities that are not so benign, where hostility, snobbery, bigotry, rigidity, threats of violence, robberies and gossip create a very unsafe environment. Inevitably, protections against these threats are evolved: cliques, alienation, ostracisation. The ultimate protection is, of course, to leave the area.

Unsafe workplaces

The atmosphere in workplaces can be unsafe in very much the same way that homes can be emotionally unsafe. Staff relationships tend to be the chief source of job dissatisfaction. Employees may be in dread of redundancy; in dread of being 'fired', threatened, criticised, physically or sexually harassed, humiliated and overworked; in dread of unfair expectations, exposure to irritability, dismissiveness, aggression and intimidation. It is small wonder then that job dissatisfaction is the most reliable predictor of heart disease and that most heart attacks occur before 9.00 a.m. on a Monday. Absenteeism, illness, perfectionism, overeagerness to please, timidity and passivity are examples of some of the protective strategies people develop in order to cope with an unpredictable, unsafe and uncaring work environment.

THE WISDOM OF PROTECTION

Your psyche is always highly aware of the need for safety and protection, not only from risks to its physical life but even more so from risks to its emotional and social well-being. As already pointed out, the prime need in our culture is to be loved and valued and when there are any threats to that *raison d'être* your psyche will find ways to protect you. The protective measures your psyche produces are highly creative and effective. But the sad reality is that if you are regularly or continuously trying to protect yourself from the possibility of failure and rejection, you cannot grow beyond the necessary protective walls you have created for yourself. Nevertheless, you would be very unwise to let go of any of these protections until you have found a level of safety where you are ready to move out and take on the necessary challenges that bring about desired changes.

Not only do your protective strategies often save you from further experiences of hurt and humiliation but they have another wise function. They alert you to the presence of wounded areas within yourself and between yourself and others that require healing. For example, when you protectively avoid intimate contact with others, the alerting message may be to do with an emotional rejection of self arising from your experiences of being rejected by your parents when you were a child. Similarly, children who have been sexually abused frequently repress these traumatic experiences so that they have no memory of the events. But as adults their psychosexual protectors (for example, 'hating sex' or being promiscuous to the point of endangering themselves) are windows into their wounded sexual selves. When safety is created, people will take on the alerting message of their protective behaviours. They will pursue the necessary actions to heal the hidden wounds and progress to greater maturity in those areas. When it remains unsafe, they will need to cling dearly to their protectors. When the healing process is embarked on, the protectors that have served the person so well will gradually be dissolved.

People who have had the benefit of an unconditional upbringing – where the home has always been a safe place to be – have no need to build protective walls. They will have achieved the ultimate safety: an unconditional acceptance and love of self and others, an independence and a love of life. Naturally, in situations of physical, sexual or emotional peril people with high self-esteem will also automatically engage in protective actions. They will also seek means to further strengthen their security, but such people will rarely stay hidden behind the walls of their protective actions.

Children start out with openness and reach out to the world in full confidence that they will be loved, cherished and nurtured. It is when this innate trust is broken, and neglect, conditionality, hurt and rejection begin to occur, that children in their vast wisdom begin to evolve means of eliminating or at least reducing further painful experiences. The child's world begins in the womb and there is growing evidence that the unsafety and uncertainty can arise there, when the mother is under considerable stress from her own insecurities and vulnerabilities.

The protective strategies children develop may persist into adulthood, even until death, unless it again becomes safe to venture forth with openness and trust in the world of parents, teachers, significant others, peers and employers. A major purpose of this book is to show how you can re-create safety for yourself as an adult and from that safe and open foundation take the emotional, social, occupational and spiritual risks that will enable you to move beyond your protective walls and bring you to a greater level of personal fulfilment.

The book is designed to take you on a journey of discovery of the amazing internal and external behaviours that your psyche creates in order to protect you from rejection, an emotional protection which, as earlier suggested, is akin to the protective means you develop in order to preserve your physical life. My belief is that the need for love and recognition is now greater than the need for preservation of physical life. Witness to this are people who have sacrificed their lives for others, for religious and political causes – all, I believe, to gain love, acceptance and recognition.

On this journey of the psyche's means of protection, you will discover that protective behaviours operate at different levels: physical (stress and illness), conscious (what you feel, think, do and say), preconscious (deeper feelings and attitudes) and subconscious (repression of traumatic experiences and fear of abandonment). You will also see that the wisest part of your psyche – the unconscious – is constantly active on your behalf to heal your inner conflicts and help you to move on to a greater realisation of your being. Furthermore, you will see that thoughts, attitudes, behaviours, feelings and illnesses that are often labelled as 'negative' have, in reality, the creative function of protecting you from threats to your emotional and social well-being. Rather than suddenly trying to let go of those so-called 'negative' behaviours, you will be encouraged to hold on to them until sufficient safety has been created for you to become venturesome again.

The book strongly contends that it is not changing your thinking that is the basis for emotional and social transformation but changing directly how you feel about yourself, about others and about the world. How this emotional process can be brought about is discussed in the later chapters of the book. Creating safety is the first and essential step in this process. From this basis you can begin to take the appropriate actions that will set you on the road to greater maturity and fulfilment. *Bon voyage*!

CHAPTER 2

THE POWER OF 'NEGATIVE' THINKING

THERE IS NO SUCH THING AS NEGATIVE THINKING

Is it true to say that there is no such thing as negative thinking? After all, many books have been written on the power of positive thinking and the detrimental nature of negative thinking. Writers who promote the practice of positive thinking suggest that the way you think determines what you feel.

I remember a time in my own life when, at social functions, I used to hide away in corners from people and on one particular occasion two young women invited me to come on out and join them. I remember clearly thinking: 'They're only saying that because they feel sorry for me and if I do accept their offer, they'll probably get bored of me quite quickly.' Had I gone to a cognitive therapist (who believes how you think determines how you feel) she would have said that my thought process was critical of myself and a misinterpretation of the invitation, leading to the continuation of the social avoidance – which is precisely what happened as I made some vague excuse to the two women and remained depressed and alone in my corner. It seems that the way I thought was indeed negative and prevented me from taking up the social opportunity. However, I find it very odd that any therapist should start out by criticising me! Furthermore, with such an approach I am given no credit for the function of the sequence of 'negative' thinking following the women's request. I believe that that pattern of thinking served a very useful and creative purpose; one which proponents of positive thinking miss. The thinking sequence served a twofold purpose:

- to project on to the women my emotional inability to respond to the request
- to protect me from rejection.

How clever! Through my thinking I had managed to project my own doubts about myself on to the two women: 'They're only saying that because they feel sorry for me' and 'they'll probably get bored of me quite quickly'. The hidden issues at the time were: 'I am feeling sorry for myself and I lack any sense of myself in relationships with women.' These are deep emotional problems – not cognitive ones. My hate of myself was very great at that time and my 'negative thinking' served the very wise purpose of protecting me from taking the risk of rejection by the two women.

My belief is that unless we resolve our own rejection of ourselves then we will continue to use the head (in the form of images and thoughts) to protect ourselves from hurt and rejection. The head protects the heart. It is not my thinking that determines how I feel, it is precisely the opposite. It is how I feel about myself, others, the world, the past, the future and the present that determines how I think. The key feeling is how I feel about myself since this colours how I feel about everything else. In the example given above, my hate of myself, primarily of my physical self, determined how I responded to the well-meant request by the two women. This hate of my physical self preceded the 'negative' thought sequence; it was not created by it. The sequence of 'negative' thoughts served as a weapon against the emotional threat of possible rejection by the two women. It is not wise to remove a weapon from someone and leave them defenceless against what they perceive as a painful and threatening world.

PROTECTIVE THINKING RATHER THAN NEGATIVE THINKING

I believe there is no such thing as negative thinking. Rather I believe that people creatively develop protective patterns of thinking to reduce the possibility of further hurt, humiliation and rejection. Let us take some typical examples of what has been considered negative thinking:

- 'I know I'll fail that exam.'
- 'I wish we didn't have to meet those people tonight.'
- 'I hate going into work today.'
- 'I look awful.'
- 'Everybody else on the course will know more than I do.'

The student who dreads failure will think in protective ways about the examination because it represents a huge threat to her self-esteem. Failure can mean rejection by both self and parents. By expecting a failure, the student is attempting to dilute the huge need for success and also to prepare for the eventuality of failure. When the student voices the thought 'I know I'm going to fail', she is attempting to alter the expectations of those who put on pressure for high performance. One young man told me that he hated when his parents had high expectations of him. No wonder. When he failed to measure up to their demanding standards he was met with the inevitable criticism and rejection. He very cleverly pointed out to me that by expressing constant worry about examinations and difficulties with concentration, he managed to reduce his parents' expectations of him. Hardly negative thinking or talking! It is more accurate to say that he had developed a cognitive strategy to protect himself from rejection by his parents.

The second example of so-called negative thinking is indicative of hidden emotional issues of social inadequacy. The 'wish we didn't have to meet these people' (covert or voiced) serves to motivate avoidance of the situation and also to prepare the person for the dreaded likelihood of feeling uncomfortable in the situation. The fulfilment of the prophecy in turn becomes an additional rationale and a strengthened protection against further social excursions of a like kind. It is important to see that the person who is self-possessed and independent of others will not dread social situations in the way that a person who has poor self-esteem and is dependent on others will. Again, the so-called negative thought pattern not only reflects the person's emotional doubts about self and consequent dependence on others, but also mobilises attempts to protect against social failure. Once again, the emotional vulnerability precedes the 'negative' thought pattern and gives rise to the necessity of a cognitive strategy to protect against the social threats to self-esteem. In this kind of situation, very often the protective thinking pattern precedes the verbalisation to another person of the reticence about the social outing. The verbalisation is a second line of protection and is designed to persuade others to forego the social invitation. Such a response would lead to the desired outcome of avoidance of the threatening social situation. There is a world of difference between an honest and open 'no' to a social invitation and the less obvious protective response to such an invitation given in the present example. The person who is dependent on others and feels vulnerable in the face of certain social situations will not readily admit to such vulnerability because this would mean risking exposure to criticism and possible rejection. It is safer to engage in behaviours that keep hidden the true emotional issues and protect against the risk of exposure. Clever, surely, and not at all negative!

A common 'negative' thought pattern is 'I hate going into work today'. Individuals who feel confident and competent do not think about their jobs in this way. When difficulties arise, they see them as challenges from which they can emerge more knowledgeable and, perhaps, wiser. The person who is unsure, afraid of the judgment of others and fearful of failure will view work in protective ways. The thought 'I hate going into work' is a projection of the person's own doubts about self on to the job. People often say 'it's the job that gets me down', not allowing themselves to see that it is their own vulnerability that makes the job so threatening. By projecting your emotional difficulties on to the job, you protect yourself from having to face your own low self-esteem (which is far too threatening to view) and when you voice your difficulties with work to others, you divert their attention away from you and on to your occupation. Again the subconscious wisdom of the psyche is apparent and it will be reluctant to let go of these protective cognitive strategies until the deeper emotional conflicts are resolved.

I can empathise deeply with the next example of 'negative' thinking: 'I look awful'. For years I struggled with a severe rejection of my physical self, seeing myself as unattractive and ugly, and avoiding contact with women. This pattern of thinking served to protect me from what I most feared – rejection. If I had followed the advice to practise positive thinking – 'I am handsome', 'I accept myself as I am', 'I am unique', 'I am independent of how others see me' – I do not feel that it would have altered my emotional conviction of my ugliness in any significant way. Furthermore, if I had dropped my protective thinking pattern and had gone ahead and asked a woman for a date and she had refused me, then the emotional reaction might indeed have been devastating. What if somebody had expressed attraction to me? Would this have resolved my self-esteem problem? This did happen a number of times but with little effect because, as an adult, emotional healing does not come about through another's expression of love for you (even though it always helps) but through the deeper process of your own love and acceptance of yourself. The protection offered by 'I look awful' is that it provides justification for avoiding contact with others and that avoidance, in turn, protects against the feared criticism and rejection of others.

The final example of 'negative' thinking – 'everybody else on the course will know more than I do' – reflects the self-esteem problem of lack of confidence and the consequent fear of 'being found out' to be less competent than others. Your thought pattern prepares you to protect yourself during attendance of the course, and by seeing others as 'superior' you allow them to take the lead while you remain quietly in the background. Many people confuse confidence with competence and believe that when you are knowledgeable and skilled in a particular task you will then feel confident. Confidence which is dependent on competence is pseudo-confidence because you are always fearful of mistakes and failures, and anxiety accompanies your actions. Take the example of learning to drive a car. Many people approach this complex skill with the thought 'I'll never be able to do it', reflecting a lack of confidence in their ability to learn. The pattern of thinking and its verbalisation serve the protective function of reducing the driving tutor's expectations of you. You may believe that, once you have accomplished the task of driving independently, you will feel confident. Not so! Confidence precedes competence. Confidence is knowing that you have the potential to learn any task and that once you apply yourself persistently you will learn the targeted knowledge and/or skill. Confidence is also knowing that, yes, you will make mistakes, but these mistakes are simply pointers for further learning.

I have been attempting to show that there is no such thing as negative thinking because such thought patterns serve the important function of protection against failure, criticism, humiliation and rejection. It is vital that individuals are given credit for the creative nature of their so-called negative thinking patterns and that they are helped to resolve the hidden emotional conflicts that make them so vulnerable. By relabelling 'negative' thinking as 'protective' thinking, the person is no longer being criticised for the way she thinks but, on the contrary, is being given recognition for the need for protection and credit for the development of the cognitive means to do so.

TYPES OF PROTECTIVE THINKING

Books written on cognitive therapy tend to categorise negative thinking into faulty judgments that people make about themselves, the world and the future. Examples of such faulty judgments are:

- Self – 'I'm a fool.'
- The world – 'Nobody loves me.'
- The future – 'Nothing will ever change.'

In cognitive therapy judgments such as these are seen as creating feelings of fear, anxiety, hate, depression, sadness, loneliness, hopelessness, despair, anger and jealousy. The duration, depth and frequency of these feelings are seen as being determined by the intensity of the faulty judgments made by the individual.

It is easy to see why a thought sequence such as 'I'm a fool' should be described as an inaccurate judgment of self. After all, you are not summed up by any one thing that you do or fail to do. A cognitive therapist would help you to see, for example, that yes, you did make an error because of lack of concentration, but that does not make you a fool. You would be encouraged to substitute the faulty judgment of 'I'm a fool' with the more realistic assessment that you made an error owing to a lapse in concentration. You can then learn from this by making a greater effort to hold your concentration on the task in hand. But with such an approach, no credit is given to the creator of the thought process and its important functions are not recognised. In fact, the thought 'I'm a fool' can have a number of protective functions.

- It reduces your own expectations of yourself, so that mistakes and failures are not the hammer blows you experienced as a child.
- When voiced, it reduces others' expectations of you by leading them to believe that only failures and mistakes can be expected from you.

A further protection is that, given their low expectations, people may be agreeably surprised when you turn out to surpass their expectations. Remember that much of this process is subconscious; your psyche constantly works to protect you from pain and also creates opportunities for you to resolve your hidden emotional problems.

When a client tells me 'I'm a fool', my response is to say: 'I can understand why you need to see yourself in that way; it is a necessary and clever means you have developed in order to protect yourself from a world that has become emotionally unsafe for you.' I help the person to see that it is not stupid, nor irrational, to think in these ways. On the contrary, such protective ways of thinking have made it possible to survive in a world wherein, as a child, conditionality or outright neglect may have been part and parcel of everyday life.

An example of the type of 'negative' thinking that involves faulty judgment about the world is 'nobody loves me'. A cognitive therapist would challenge your judgment and help you to see that there are, in reality, individuals who demonstrate caring behaviour towards you. Again, in this example it is easy to understand how it is concluded that your thinking is inaccurate and that the help needed is to correct such faulty judgments of how others see you. A cognitive therapist would see the thinking pattern as the problem, whereas I am suggesting that thoughts are both manifestations and protectors of deeper emotional issues. The thoughts are not the problem and the target of change must go behind the scenes of protective thinking patterns. When a person thinks or declares 'nobody loves me', the protective functions of this judgment process may include the following:

- □ It projects your own lack of love of self on to others. Projection has the very intelligent purpose of taking the focus away from yourself and on to another so that you do not have to face your own emotional vulnerability.
- □ It invites a sympathetic response from others, a protest that such is not the case and, sometimes, it provokes an increased effort on other people's part to reassure you.
- □ It reduces your own emotional expectations of others so that disappointment and hurt are reduced if affection is not forthcoming from others.
- □ It provides a rationale for not taking the risk of expressing emotional needs.

I recall working with a young mother of four children who told me once that she 'hated' her children and her husband. She expressed deep guilt about these feelings. I reassured her that I had no doubt that there were very good reasons why she thought and felt in these ways about her children and partner. The protective function gradually began to emerge when she declared: 'I don't see how my children or husband could ever love me.' By hating her children and husband, she protected herself from what she saw as their inevitable rejection of her. Other protective thinking present was that she saw herself as a 'bad mother and wife'; this had the functions of not having to face into her deeply troubled self and the reduction of her own and others' expectations of her as mother and spouse. Only when she learned to love and value herself did she let go of the protective cognitive and emotional behaviours she had displayed through most of her married life.

An example of the third type of 'negative' thinking, involving faulty judgments about the future, is 'nothing will ever change'. A cognitive therapist would help a client with such a thought to see that this is a very dismal, pessimistic and faulty way of evaluating the future. She would then help the client to see that a more rational view would be that many things do change and that there is no reason why specific changes cannot occur in the client's future. This seems logical, but again the person is being given no credit for the creativity and meaning of the thought. There is 'method to the madness' in that the following protective functions may be operating:

- Projection of your own helplessness on to the future so that you do not have to face the sad reality of your own emotional vulnerability.
- Provision of a rationale for avoidance of constructive action that threatens your hidden insecurity.
- Creation of the possibility of a sympathetic response from others and the possibility that they will take responsibility for you, thereby eliminating any need for risk-taking on your part.

□ Reduction of your own expectations of the future so that if things do go wrong, you can quickly protect yourself with 'I wouldn't have expected anything else'.

Performance anxiety about events, such as an examination, dinner party or public speech, provides a good example of the protective nature of worrying about the future. Many people get terribly stressed when guests are coming to dinner. They fuss, worry and may even panic about how the evening will turn out. They are attempting to protect themselves from failure and criticism. They are not being negative but protective.

IDENTIFYING YOUR PATTERNS OF PROTECTIVE THINKING

Protective thinking patterns not only provide you with emotional protection but are also a window into the hidden world of your emotional vulnerability. As such, they provide you with an opportunity to resolve these problems.

It is useful then to be able to identify the patterns of protective thinking you may be practising as a first step in taking up the challenge of overcoming your emotional insecurities. These patterns can be described under the following headings:

□ self
□ others
□ the world
□ the future
□ the past.

Protective thoughts about self

If experiences in childhood have seriously undermined your concept of yourself, the following are examples of how you may be protectively thinking about yourself:

- ☐ 'I'm stupid.'
- ☐ 'I'm despicable.'
- ☐ 'I'm ugly.'
- ☐ 'I'm bad.'
- ☐ 'I'm useless and worthless.'
- ☐ 'I'm never good enough.'
- ☐ 'I'm average.'
- ☐ 'I'm less than others.'
- ☐ 'I'm lazy.'
- ☐ 'I'm a bad mother (or father).'
- ☐ 'I'm the black sheep of the family.'
- ☐ 'I'm perfect.' ('superiority' protective strategy)
- ☐ 'I'm never wrong.' ('superiority' protective strategy)

In these self-statements introjection (internalising what other people say about you) is the dominant protective strategy: either 'I'm so bad' that nothing could be expected of me and I have justification for avoiding risk-taking, or 'I'm so good' that I work and work and work to maintain other people's acceptance of me. Any threat to my 'superiority' concept of myself may quickly result in a shift from overeffort to the opposite type of introjection which is the strategy of avoidance: with no effort, there can be no failure; with no failure, no humiliation and rejection.

Protective thoughts about others

When you are emotionally vulnerable to rejection by others, a clever strategy is to project your rejection of yourself on to others in either a general or a specific manner. Examples of thinking patterns arising from such projection are:

- ☐ 'Nobody cares.'
- ☐ 'People are full of shit.'

- ☐ 'People think only about themselves.'
- ☐ 'You're so selfish.'
- ☐ 'You're never here when I need you.'
- ☐ 'You're rigid and aggressive.'
- ☐ 'You never see my needs.'
- ☐ 'You think you're great, don't you?'
- ☐ 'You can't trust anyone anymore.'

It is not difficult to detect the covert emotional issues behind these blaming messages. If you change the third person or the 'you' in the message to an 'I', the inner conflict is often revealed:

- ☐ 'I don't care for myself.'
- ☐ 'I'm full of shit (hurt, rejection).'
- ☐ 'I have not established a life of my own.'
- ☐ 'I don't think enough of myself.'
- ☐ 'I'm not here for myself.'
- ☐ 'I'm rigid and aggressive.'
- ☐ 'I never see my own needs.'
- ☐ 'I don't think I'm great at all.'
- ☐ 'I don't trust myself to take care of myself.'

The major protection in projection is that, by putting the focus on the other, you do not have to face up to your own vulnerability. Neither do you have to take any emotional risks when you engage in projection because when you think like this about others, the onus is put on them to change rather than on you.

Protective thoughts about the world

Children develop tremendous security when through having their physical, emotional, social and other needs met regularly they learn that the world is an orderly, predictable and caring place to be. However, when children's needs are not attended to regularly, then they begin to protect themselves and they see the world as a fundamentally unsafe place to be. In seeing the world in this way children, and later on adults, protect themselves and they now take few risks in exploring the richness of the world. I have worked with individuals who believed that if they stepped outside their front door, some awful disaster would befall. Avoidance behaviours, severe phobias, emotional and physical withdrawal are all revelations of a child's emotional insecurities. The child will wisely hold on to these ways of viewing the world until at least the beginnings of some emotional security develop. Examples of protective thoughts about the world are:

- 'Nobody is safe anymore.'
- 'What's good about the world?'
- 'Life is meaningless.'
- 'The world is in a terrible state.'
- 'It's not safe to travel anymore.'
- 'That person is living in a fool's paradise.'
- 'People aren't safe in their own beds.'
- 'Life is just a series of problems.'
- 'Who'd want to live long in this world?'
- 'The world is the same all over.'
- 'You wouldn't get me going up in an aeroplane.'
- 'Stick to what you know is what I say.'
- 'The devil you know is better than the one you don't know.'
- 'I won't be sorry to leave this world.'

It is clear that all these pessimistic thoughts protect you from having to take any risks. But the sad thing is that because of the need for protection you have lost the love of challenge, the natural curiosity and eagerness to learn that is so evident in toddlers. Somehow, your experiences have taught you that it is better to play it safe, be apathetic or steer a middle path through life. The protection of pessimism is needed to justify your safety-seeking lack of action until the time and circumstances are ripe for you to create safety and security within yourself.

Protective thoughts about the future

When you are vulnerable, you tend to live in the future or in the past, or both. A reliable indicator of inner security is the ability to focus on the here and now. Many concentration difficulties stem from anticipatory protective thinking where you worry about what may or may not happen in the future. This worrying serves the function of keeping you vigilant to happenings that may threaten your self-esteem. For example, if you feel you have to be the perfect parent, then you may find yourself worrying constantly that the welfare of your child is being looked after properly. I have worked with parents who put themselves under considerable strain by having their children with them all the time, resisting any suggestion that they take a break or get a baby-minder. They subconsciously believe: 'If I keep worrying, then I am less likely to forget particular welfare actions that my child needs and so I'll be the perfect parent.' These parents are terrified of failure and of mistakes, and by living in the future they have found a strategy to guard against any possible slip of responsibility.

Living in the future may also guard against failure because by predicting disaster you are preparing yourself for such eventualities. Again, of course, in addition to its protective function this pattern of thinking has the added function of alerting you to your hidden, unresolved, emotional conflicts. Commonly used protective thoughts about the future include:

- □ 'I know I'll fail.'
- □ 'I'll look a mess this evening.'
- □ 'Things never work out for me.'
- □ 'I have so much to do tomorrow.'
- □ 'How will I cope when you're away?'
- □ 'I won't be able to stop worrying.'
- □ 'Why did I agree to give this party?'
- □ 'I know I won't sleep tonight with worrying about the children.'
- □ 'I'll hate when the children start school.'
- □ 'Bad things are always happening to me.'
- □ 'Nothing will ever change.'
- □ 'I'm dreading going into my new job on Monday.'
- □ 'I lie awake every night thinking about you.'
- □ 'I'll always be alone.'

All these thoughts are examples of introjection whereby you have internalised messages of doubts about your capability and/or lovability from others. These introjected messages propel you into protective compensatory actions of worrying, fretting and perfectionism. Such protections are necessary until you find the safety to get in touch with your wondrous person and immense capability.

Protective thoughts about the past

While living in the future is the outcome of introjected messages about lack of capability, living in the past, by contrast, is often indicative of projection, whereby you blame the past for your current low sense of yourself. By projecting on to the past, you protect yourself from having to take responsibility for the present. Examples of this process are:

- □ 'Given my past, what would you expect of me?'
- □ 'My parents never cared for me.'

- □ 'School was just a washout.'
- □ 'It's no wonder I am the way I am when you see my parents.'
- □ 'The Church made fools out of us.'
- □ 'Teachers never liked me.'
- □ 'My parents never had time for me.'
- □ 'That person who sexually abused me has ruined my life.'
- □ 'My education never did me any good.'
- □ 'My parents have ruined my life.'

Living in the past can also involve introjection, whereby you blame yourself for things that happened back then. In reliving old hurts or failures, you are like a child picking at a scab, but the protective function of such reliving is to guard against a repeat of the uncomfortable experiences. Examples of this process are:

- □ 'I feel so embarrassed when I think of what I said to those people last night.'
- □ 'After what happened, I never want to see these people again.'
- □ 'How could I have let myself down so much?'
- □ 'I must have been a horrible child.'
- □ 'I don't know how anyone could have ever loved me.'

The last two examples reveal introjection of very serious rejection experiences and provide protection against any further rejection by justifying avoidance of reaching out emotionally and socially to others.

CHAPTER 3

THE POWER OF 'POSITIVE' THINKING

THERE IS NO SUCH THING AS POSITIVE THINKING

Many therapists – most famously Norman Vincent Peale – have put major emphasis on the practice of positive thinking as a means of changing how you feel about yourself, others, the world, the future and the past. In spite of the influence which books such as *The Power of Positive Thinking* have had on people's lives, I believe that the term 'positive thinking' is a misnomer.

Thinking is like the weather: in itself it is neither good nor bad. However, when people project their own needs and feelings on to the weather, then the weather can become 'good' to one person and 'bad' to another: a farmer who is crying out for rain will see the persistent sunshine as 'bad', while the holidaymaker will see the same sunshine as 'glorious' and the dark clouds as 'bad'. Similarly, thoughts in themselves have little power to influence how people feel about themselves, or others, or life; it is the emotions which infuse them that are powerful.

I recall one client who had a deep hatred of herself and who had paranoid thoughts that other people were constantly saying 'bad' things about her. She also felt that others could see evil in her face and, as a result, avoided approaching her. Through my unconditional love and acceptance of her, she gradually began to see that she had developed a very powerful means of keeping people at bay and so was effectively managing to protect herself from the hurt she anticipated in relationships. I told her that I fully understood that her 'paranoid' thinking was necessary and that she would not be wise to let go of her protective armour until the hidden emotional turmoil of her hatred of herself was resolved. I discovered that her mother had been unable to show any love towards her and had regularly displayed feelings of irritability, anger and hate. These feelings were manifested through constant criticism, physical beatings and aggressive outbursts. It took a year to help this client to let go of her need to project on to others her childhood experiences of rejection and her own non-acceptance of herself. The safety to let go of her protection came about only through the unconditional love shown in the therapeutic relationship and her own eventual internalisation of this love. Change came not through developing more positive thoughts, but through love, which gave her the safety she needed.

In the same way 'positive' words from another in themselves will have no power for change unless infused with emotion. For instance if a child has written a wonderful essay and I say to him 'You're a great boy', but I make no eye-contact with the child and the remark is made in a throwaway fashion, without sincerity or warmth, the child will not benefit from my praise of his achievement. However, if I make warm eye-contact with the child and express my delight in my words, then I have no doubt that the child will feel good about himself.

Take another example where you are feeling insecure about whether your partner truly loves you. You express your insecurity with the question: 'Helen, are you sure you love me?' and you get the response, 'Of course I love you', but it is accompanied with a dismissive wave of the hands and irritation in the voice. Are you convinced? Hardly! The words are positive, 'Of course I love you', but because they are not infused with love, sincerity and concern over your doubts, you are left feeling even more insecure than before you asked the question.

Thoughts and words are but vehicles for emotions in your relationship with yourself and in your relationships with others and, unless the appropriate feelings accompany the thoughts and words, their influence will be indirect and minimal. My belief is that when the love feelings are present, the positive thoughts will automatically follow. In my own experience, and in my experience of working with people who possess no caring feelings for themselves and are infected with hate and rejection of self, neither positive thinking nor expressions of affection and warmth from others penetrate the protective walls that had to be built up to guard against experiences of hurt.

There are many deeply depressed people who are loved by others, but who cannot let in the love messages; it would be far too risky to do so since the danger is that the love could be quickly withdrawn and they would find themselves plunged back into darkness. There is another, deeper, issue here: if, for example, I have seen myself for years as despicable, unlovable, stupid, useless, worthless, ugly, unattractive, how can I suddenly accept the opposite? It is safer to protect myself rather than take the risks that follow by letting in the love message. Too often during my own years of depression, I twisted the loving messages people sent me with such protective rationalisations as:

- 'They're only saying that because they feel sorry for me.'
- 'If they really knew me, they wouldn't say that.'
- 'I wonder what that person wants from me?'
- 'Surely they don't expect me to believe that?'

The rejection feelings within myself were like a foaming sea compared to the dew drop of kindness in the words of another. It takes a lot more than words to break through to the massively defended heart of a person with low self-esteem.

The power of non-verbal communication is a further illustration that words or thoughts do not determine how people feel about themselves. It is not words, for example, that convince infants that they are loved, but the expression in the parents' eyes, the facial expression, the gentle touch, the silent holding, the caressing, the smiling, the feeding, the comforting, the nurturing, the listening, the response to needs. Without the regular expression of love in all these non-verbal ways, nothing, not even 'positive' words, will convince children that they are loved. Somehow we recognise that the directly emotional ways of relating to children are the most effective ways of raising self-esteem. However, when it comes to resolving our emotional insecurity as adults, we tend to go into our heads rather than heal our hearts. The head is very far from the heart, and being stuck in your head is a clever means of avoiding the emotional encounters that so threaten your heart.

OPEN THINKING RATHER THAN POSITIVE THINKING

I have suggested that there is no such thing as positive thinking because the label 'positive' implies that it is the thinking which is the medium for change, whereas it is the feelings with which it is infused that are the real source of power. A more accurate label for such thinking would be 'open' thinking. When I can receive the feelings expressed in such affirmations as 'I love you', or 'I love myself', or 'I am capable', or 'I enjoyed being with you', it means that I am 'open' to my own worth and value. The open thinking used as a medium for expressing feelings is the beam of light that connects with the inner light of your own loving and valuing feelings of yourself. As you have seen, when you are shut off from others' expressions of feelings towards you or cannot respond to rehearsal of positive thoughts, this reflects the darkness within yourself; to protect yourself, you must remain closed off to any feelings, however expressed, from others and yourself until light is brought to bear on the inner darkness.

I do not wish to suggest that people should not practise positive thinking, but I am emphasising the deeper emotional process that is needed if people want to change. Open thinking is an important medium for feelings and can reinforce the internal valuing and loving of self which occurs within individuals who have high self-esteem. But people who seriously devalue and reject themselves are unlikely to benefit from open thinking because it would be too risky for them to utter or receive an open verbal expression of care from another or from themselves.

TYPES OF OPEN THINKING

As with types of protective thinking outlined in the last chapter, open thinking can be about:

- □ self
- □ parents
- □ significant others
- □ the present
- □ the past
- □ the future
- □ life itself.

Open thoughts about self

As an adult, how you feel about yourself determines all your internal and external behaviours towards yourself, others, work and life. When you feel deep acceptance of yourself, your thoughts will automatically reflect that maturity. However, there are relatively few people who have attained these heights of self-esteem and, as you saw in the last chapter, our thoughts are more likely to reflect self-rejection. If you possess some sense of your own worth, then certainly practice of the following open statements about yourself will strengthen and enhance your feelings of love and acceptance of yourself:

- □ 'I love and accept myself.'
- □ 'I am deeply aware of my goodness and worth.'
- □ 'I wonder at my uniqueness.'
- □ 'I have limitless capabilities.'
- □ 'I am determined to nurture, value and respect myself at all times.'
- □ 'My behaviour does not reflect my worth as a person.'
- □ 'I am responsible for all my actions towards myself, others and the world.'
- □ 'I am responsible for getting my own needs met.'
- □ 'I accept only real goals and values for myself.'
- □ 'I value my independence.'

If, when reading these open thoughts on self, you feel 'uncomfortable', 'stupid', 'angry', 'foolish', 'nervous', 'giggly' or 'tearful', please respect these feelings as being protective of your well-being. If these feelings continue, it is advisable not to persist with rehearsing these thoughts but to seek the help and safety you need in order to resolve your underlying feelings of self-rejection.

Open thoughts about parents

There is a common saying that parents have a lot to answer for, and it is not surprising that many of our thoughts as adults (and, indeed, as children) about our parents can seem of a condemning nature. On the other hand, your thoughts on your parents may paint a rosy picture, even though your poor self-image belies the loving messages of your thoughts and statements about your childhood. This is a clever protection system, a reaction formation that depicts the opposite of what really happened and guards against having to face the sad reality of a painful childhood.

Much safety is required before individuals will be ready to let go of such fantasies about their parents. When we have seemingly condemning and critical thoughts about our parents, what we are doing is projecting our problems on to our parents, thereby protecting ourselves from the threatening tasks of facing up to our own weaknesses and vulnerabilities. Our parents did their best. No matter how difficult a life they created for us, given their personal insecurities and interpersonal difficulties, they did not have the emotional safety and maturity to act in any other way. While they are not to blame, their actions nevertheless are responsible for our problems as adults. But as adults the responsibility for change now lies with us, not with them. People talk about 'forgiving' parents, but I do not believe any forgiving is necessary.

My parents did not deliberately abandon and abuse me. Their behaviour towards me was caused by the hidden depths of the abuse they themselves experienced as children, and unwittingly perpetuated as adults. It is not forgiveness that is required but compassion. When you look in the mirror of your own sad history of neglect, criticism, ridicule, unfair expectations, conditional loving, outright rejection, or physical, sexual or emotional abuse, you also have reflected back to you your parents' history. Both my parents died in their early sixties and it is my regret that my own healing had not occurred before their deaths. I can now feel immense compassion for and understanding of their hidden hurt, weaknesses, fears and vulnerabilities. My feelings of blame, rage, anger and resentment have been transformed into love, compassion and acceptance. At least I can now share these feelings with other members of my family, with my partner, friends, clients and anybody whose path crosses mine.

There are those who react against such compassionate understanding and are concerned that I am excusing the neglectful actions of parents and others. Actually, it is quite the contrary. I am very clear with parents that, although they are in no way to blame when a child is deeply troubled, their actions nonetheless are responsible for the child's plight. It is important then, and I am very firm on this, that they now face the troubled lives within themselves so that they can reach the level of emotional safety and maturity that will provide the ground for their child's healthy development in the future.

The following are some examples of compassionate and loving thoughts on parents that you may like to try out:

- □ 'I know my parents did their best for me.'
- □ 'I can see now their insecurities and vulnerabilities and am accepting of their life struggles, even though these had deep effects on me.'
- □ 'I love my parents.'
- □ 'I feel compassion for them.'
- □ 'I am independent of and separate from them.'
- □ 'I take the responsibility to heal any hurts and experiences of rejection suffered in childhood.'
- □ 'I am not responsible for my parents but want to be supportive when they genuinely need help.'
- □ 'For their sakes as well as my own sake, I will no longer collude with their attempts to dominate or overprotect me.'
- □ 'I can now stand on my own two capable feet and not be dependent on them.'

- ☐ 'I am letting go of the parent–child relationship I have had with them.'
- ☐ 'I want to establish an adult-to-adult friendship with them.'
- ☐ 'I respect their differences from me in values, morals and life perspective.'
- ☐ 'I can be myself when I visit my parents.'
- ☐ 'I have a right to be different from them.'

Once again, if on reading these suggestions for open thoughts on your parents you feel rage, anger, sadness, despair, depression or numbness, it is important that you respect and value these feelings and see them as creative and protective messages regarding the need for greater emotional safety before you are ready to infuse the suggestions with genuine love and compassion. Seek out that safety, for yourself most of all, because you are carrying emotional baggage that needs unloading, but also for your parents, because they need your love and compassion as much as you deserve it from them. Do not persist with these statements against the tide of your protective feelings, but do act to acquire safety.

Open thoughts about significant others

When I was a child, aunts and uncles had quite an influence on our family. My mother was invalided when I was six years of age and, as a result, they tended to visit a lot. I am a twin and when they came, they never wanted to take me out but always took my twin brother. This happened despite the fact that I was the 'goodie-good' child who made them tea and generally tried to please them. Children always blame themselves when they are not liked and assume that there is something wrong with them. I assumed I was ugly and unattractive and that they were ashamed to be seen with me. This assumption was reinforced by their overt admiration of how handsome my brother was (we are not identical twins!). One aunt in particular deepened the wound. When I was six years of age she told me: 'Some day maybe you'll be as good-looking as your brother.' These early messages made it unsafe for me to be with relatives, and I quickly learned to protect myself through feeling resentful and making as little contact with them as possible.

There are many people who have suffered far worse rejection from relatives, teachers, child-minders or brothers and sisters. Grand-parents, aunts and uncles who have obvious favourites seriously undermine the self-esteem of the children who are ignored. Some of my adult clients have experienced physical or sexual abuse at the hands of relatives or child-minders. Teachers have made life hell for many children. My own twin brother hated school because of feeling put down and being physically abused. He left school at thirteen years of age, and even though he now makes a lot more money than I do, he has a 'hang-up' from those school days and is convinced that I am the intelligent one and that he lacks intelli-gence. I have worked with individuals who, even after twenty, thirty, forty years, have huge rage towards teachers who humiliated them. Many of my clients also have suffered at the hands of older brothers or sisters and have carried these estranged relationships into adulthood.

As in the case of parents, these people who so affected our lives did not do so deliberately, but were acting out unwittingly from their own hurt and neglected childhoods. Again, while compassion and understanding of their behaviour are needed, collusion needs to stop. The following suggestions for open thoughts may go some way towards healing your relationships with significant others whether in your past or in your present life.

- □ 'I accept, value and respect the person of significant others in my life.'
- □ 'Where significant others show unacceptable behaviours towards me or others, I will gently and firmly confront them.'
- □ 'I am separate from and independent of the significant people in my life both in the here and now and in the past.'
- □ 'I feel compassion for them and see their behaviour as springing from their hidden insecurities.'
- □ 'I wish them happiness and contentment.'
- □ 'I wish to have an adult relationship with them.'
- □ 'I will hold on to my right to be different from them.'
- □ 'I will no longer allow them to impose artificial values on me.'
- □ 'I respect their right to be different from me.'
- □ 'I let go of needing approval and acceptance from them.'

If, when reading these open thoughts on significant people in your life, you feel calmness, compassion, love, acceptance, understanding, or if you feel that emotions of resentment, bitterness, anger, rage are beginning to recede, then persist with the thoughts. However, if these latter feelings remain strong, it is wise to stop practising the suggested thoughts and to seek out the emotional safety and healing that will help you to resolve the conflicts underlying the feelings.

Open thoughts about the present

When we are insecure, we have difficulty living in the present: we tend to protect ourselves by either projecting into the future or living in the past. However, present-moment living is an essential aspect of healing ourselves. When we focus on the 'now', it means all our energies and resources are available to us and can be effectively applied to the activity in hand. The following suggestions for open thoughts are designed as cues to help you to focus totally on what you are doing at present. If, in spite of these cues, you keep finding yourself wandering into the past or future, then this is a clear indication that far deeper emotional work is needed for you to be able to let go of your protective thinking pattern.

- □ 'Life is here and now.'
- □ 'I am determined to keep my mind on the present-moment activity.'
- □ 'I am far more effective when I stay in the present.'
- □ 'I want to be fully present when I give time to myself.'
- □ 'I want to be fully present when relating to others.'
- □ 'I give myself totally to living in the present.'
- □ 'Living in the present is one of the best gifts I can give myself.'
- □ 'Everything I need is to be found here in the present.'

Open thoughts about the past

There are many people who find protection in living in the past. Some view the past through rose-tinted glasses and cleverly avoid facing up to the realities of the present. There are others who can amuse you endlessly with story after story about the past but by doing so manage to never allow you to get emotionally close – an efficient distance regulator. There are still others who blame the past for all their problems. This is also an avoidance strategy. By projecting all your difficulties on to the past, you do not have to take on the responsibility for change. Your past does, indeed, colour your present but no change or growth can occur if you protectively bury your head in the sand of the past. Safety is needed for you to be able to get beyond your past. When you possess some degree of safety, the following suggestions for open thoughts about the past will connect you more deeply with your worth and resources for change and help you to see the past in a more mature way:

- □ 'I learn from the past.'
- □ 'Mistakes and failures are opportunities for learning.'
- □ 'Success and failure are relative terms.'
- □ 'I am determined to keep from the past whatever was affirming of me and to let go of that which blocked my mature growth.'
- □ 'I will not repeat the hurtful behaviours of the past towards either myself or others.'
- □ 'My past is the stepping stone to knowing how best to be and not be here in the present.'

Once again, do not persist with rehearsal of these suggestions if any protective feelings such as anger, bitterness, sadness or loneliness well up within you. Value the message in these feelings and reach out for the safety you need in order to progress in life and leave behind the past.

Open thoughts about the future

If people can escape into the past, they can equally escape into the future, through either fantasy or anxiety. Expressions such as 'faraway hills are green', 'building castles in the air', 'the grass is greener on the other side', 'there's always tomorrow' are all indicative of a protective hope that the future will bring the security and happiness that is not here in the present. Fantasising about the future, where you create an unreal world, acts as both an avoidance of and a compensation for a real world that is too painful and too unsafe for you to take any emotional and social risks. Worrying about the future is yet another protective compensatory strategy through which you reduce any possibility of failure or disapproval, or of letting yourself down. The fear of failure and rejection catapults you into fretful actions that attempt to guard against such failure experiences. In reading the following suggestions for open thinking about the future, the feelings that arise will give you an idea of the level of your insecurity; if it is of a deep and severe nature, do not continue rehearsing these thoughts because much deeper emotional change is needed before you will be ready to internalise these suggestions.

- □ 'My present is my future.'
- □ 'I caringly plan effective use of my precious time.'
- □ 'Time management with regard to my needs and responsibilities is my way of letting myself know how worthy I am.'
- □ 'The richness of the harvest of the future is determined by how well I plant the seeds of love, hope and responsibility here in the present.'
- □ 'No matter what the future brings, I will never lose sight of my goodness and worth.'
- □ 'Happiness and fulfilment are to be found within myself.'
- □ 'It is not time that changes us but action in the here and now.'
- □ 'It is not age nor education that brings happiness or wisdom, but love of self, others and life.'

Open thoughts about life

When you are secure and independent, life is precious, mysterious, challenging, endlessly stimulating; you find that there is never enough time to do all the things you want to do; you seize every moment as if it were your last; you awaken with excitement and treasure another day's living. When you live in an unsafe world – whether external or internal or both – then life is threatening, painful, depressing, frightening, uncertain, unpredictable. When your experience of the world is like this, your thoughts reflect this sad reality and act wisely to protect you. Until both your internal and external worlds become safe, you need as much protection as you can get and you are wise not to venture out until you feel some solid ground beneath your feet. I sincerely wish that the following suggestions for open thoughts about life hold true for you, and that social, personal and interpersonal actions may bring you to a place where you can voice these thoughts from a deep inner liberation:

- □ 'Life is endlessly challenging.'
- □ 'Life is meaningful.'
- □ 'Life is mysterious.'
- □ 'It is good to be alive.'
- □ 'Life is there for me to experience in all its vast richness.'
- □ 'Life is precious.'
- □ 'I respect and value my own life and that of others.'
- □ 'I wonder at the vastness and richness of the universe.'
- □ 'I am a meaningful part of this universe.'
- □ 'I take care of the world I live in.'

PRAISE AND AFFIRMATION

Open thinking about yourself or others may be expressed in praise and affirmation.

Praise and affirmation are not the same

Though the two terms are often used interchangeably, praise and affirmation are not the same. Praise is a cognitive or verbal recognition of some action on your own part or on the part of another. Affirmation is also a cognitive or verbal recognition, but of a person and not of an action. Praise is the food that feeds responsible effort. Affirmation is the gold that enriches self-esteem. Praise then is always directed to an action. For example:

- 'John, I really appreciate that you tidied up the room after playing.'
- 'Mary, thanks for typing that letter so efficiently and promptly.'
- 'Kevin, I am really happy with the effort you are putting into your schoolwork.'
- 'Margaret, thank you for being on time for our appointment.'

In giving praise, it is best to put the emphasis on the effort rather than performance. The most common anxiety in our modern culture is performance anxiety, which is due to the tendency of parents, teachers, employers and others to provide praise only for the perfect performance, rather than for the effort put into the action. Such emphasis on performance leads to the loss among children of their natural curiosity and their love of learning, and causes them to develop protective behaviours such as avoidance, compensation, rebelliousness or apathy to guard against failure.

The target of an affirmation is the person. Affirmations take effect only when they are:

- unconditional (conditional affirmation is manipulation)
- genuine and sincere (coming from the heart and not the head).

Examples of affirmations towards others or self are:

- 'I love you.'
- 'I believe in you.'
- 'I trust in your ability to take care of yourself.'
- 'I just want to hold you.'
- 'You are wonderful.'
- 'You are precious.'
- 'You are unique.'
- 'You are free to be yourself.'
- 'You never cease to amaze me.'

- □ 'You are beautiful.'
- □ 'I value and respect myself.'
- □ 'I wonder at my unique being.'
- □ 'I love myself.'
- □ 'I am capable.'
- □ 'I am free to be myself.'

Many people have difficulty in separating person from behaviour and will say: 'After all, how can I know you if not through your behaviour?' My answer is that if you look only at my behaviour, what you will then know is not me, but the sum of my behaviours. Some of the confusion lies in regarding the words 'person' and 'personality' as synonymous. My personality is my unique person plus all my behaviours. What then is my person? I have always been struck by God's answer to Moses' question, 'Who are you Lord?', when He said: 'I am who I am.' He did not say, I am the creator of the world, or I can do this or that. Those behaviours would not have even remotely defined 'being'. The answer was perfect: 'I am who I am.' Nothing can add to or detract from this. It is the same for us human beings; each of us is a unique phenomenon in this universe, never to be repeated. 'You are who you are' and no behaviour can add to or take away from the sacredness of your being. Affirmations celebrate the being, not the doing, of people. They are emotional expressions whose presence reinforces children's sense of their wonder and whose absence leads to profound unsafety, insecurity and untold hardship for children, and adults too, if the lack of affirmations is not redressed.

Self-praise is the only praise!

In some cultures you are told you have 'a swelled head' if you say something good about yourself. Yet, if I as an adult depend on others to praise and encourage my efforts and attainments, I remain as a child tied to others and unable to operate without such positive feedback.

Praise has effect only when you internalise the approval. More often than not, you may dismiss, dilute or twist praise from others. The dismissal may occur through such cognitive reactions as: 'he doesn't really mean that', or 'if he really knew me, he wouldn't say things like that', or 'I really pulled the wool over his eyes'. Similarly, you may dilute praise by such internal statements as: 'it was nothing really', or 'anybody could do it', or 'I was just lucky really'. Twisting praise is not at all uncommon and is exemplified in such thoughts as: 'what is she after now?', or 'she's really trying to make a fool out of me and I'm not having any of it', or 'stop trying to flatter me'. When you respond in any of these ways to praise, it is an attempt to keep all the power in your hands. It is not yet safe enough for you to internalise the open feedback; it is safer to remain closed off to it. When you can graciously receive praise with a 'thank you', or 'I really appreciate your comments', or 'it makes a difference to me that you like what I've done', this reveals a level of safety and security that allows you to internalise the praise. This is why I say praise from another is self-praise: it has to pass through your screening process before it has an effect.

It is even more powerful when you can realistically appreciate, encourage and praise your own efforts. You need to become your own best friend, who believes in your capability and responds strongly to your efforts. You can always be there in this encouraging way for yourself. As an adult you no longer need to depend on others for your self-esteem. Praise from others is a wonderful bonus (when you are in a safe position to internalise it), but it is not something you look for nor do you wait around for it to occur. In this way self-praise is, indeed, the only praise.

Self-affirmation is an act of selflessness!

In the Catholic culture in which I was reared, it was drilled into us that to love oneself was selfish. One of the seven deadly sins was self-love. This teaching undermined the self-esteem of many people and, ironically, runs contrary to the fundamental message of Christianity which is to love yourself. Christ's message was so clear: 'All laws are put aside; what man needs to do is love God with all his heart and love his neighbour as he loves himself.' Psalm VIII of the Old Testament says: 'Thank you Lord for the wonder of my being.'

What defines selfishness? Surely behaviours such as dominating, controlling, manipulating, attention-seeking, aggressiveness, only seeing your own needs, blaming, criticising and judging are examples of selfishness? But it is only people who have not learned to affirm and love themselves who engage in such protective 'selfish' behaviours; they have not got a sense of their own lovability, uniqueness and vast capability to be able to see the wonder of other persons and be loving and respectful towards them. When you fully appreciate and can affirm your own being, you automatically will be loving not only of yourself but also of all others. It is through our actions of loving ourselves that we can convince others of their wonder and the wonder of the universe.

It was a strange teaching that taught denial of self and acceptance of others. Such teaching was doomed to failure because all love for others and the world springs from the well of your own love for yourself. The greatest and most powerful self-affirmation you can give yourself is: 'I love myself.' From that solid foundation you can then give the greatest affirmation to another: 'I love you.' Self-affirmation then becomes a true act of selflessness.

CHAPTER 4

THE POWER OF 'NEGATIVE' ATTITUDES

CONSCIOUS THINKING AND PRECONSCIOUS ATTITUDES

Conscious thinking refers to the thoughts you are aware of having before, during or after an activity or interaction. For example, when you awake in the morning you may be aware that you immediately begin to dread going into work, thinking to yourself: 'I wish I didn't have to face into work today' (protective thinking). Conversely, you may look forward to going into work (open thinking). During the day while at work you may engage in clock-watching and be protectively thinking: 'I hate being here and wish the time would go faster.' On the other hand you may engage in open thinking: 'I'm really enjoying the challenges the day is bringing me.' After work, you may breathe a sigh of relief while saying to yourself: 'I thought I'd never get through the day'; or, if you are secure in yourself, you may think: 'I'm pleased with what I managed to get done today.' Clearly the person who engages in the protective thinking is reflecting vulnerability and the person who engages in open thinking is reflecting confidence and competence. But, whether open or protective, these conscious thinking patterns are determined by deeper preconscious attitudes.

Take the example above where the person makes the following *protective self-statements*:

- ☐ 'I wish I didn't have to face into work today.'
- ☐ 'I hate being here and wish the time would go faster.'
- ☐ 'I thought I'd never get through the day.'

Why is this person thinking so protectively about work? The reason may be traced to preconscious attitudes that unwittingly are determining conscious thinking. Examples of such *preconscious attitudes* are:

- ☐ 'I should never make mistakes.'
- ☐ 'Everybody should like me.'
- ☐ 'I should be perfect.'
- ☐ 'I'm incapable.'
- ☐ 'Everybody else knows more than I do.'

Likewise, open thinking comes from preconscious open attitudes. In our example, the person engaging in *open thinking* made the following self-statements:

- ☐ 'I'm looking forward to the day.'
- ☐ 'I'm really enjoying the challenges the day is bringing me.'
- ☐ 'I'm pleased with what I managed to get done today.'

These open conscious thoughts are a product of *deeper open attitudes to oneself* such as:

- ☐ 'I believe in my capability to learn.'
- ☐ 'My worth is independent of success or failure.'
- ☐ 'I do not have to prove myself to others to be accepted.'
- ☐ 'Mistakes are opportunities for learning.'

If your conscious thinking is open rather than protective, you may be aware of its deeper source in preconscious open attitudes. However, when you engage in protective conscious thinking, it is far less likely that you are aware of the underlying preconscious source; this lack of awareness guards against having to face the threatening truth of your vulnerability. The person who consciously thinks in open ways has no need of such safeguards.

The preconscious attitudes that determine your conscious activities of thinking, feeling, saying and doing are often labelled as 'irrational' or 'rational' in much the same way that conscious thinking is seen as 'negative' or 'positive'. But, as for thoughts and feelings, the more appropriate terms are, I believe, 'open' and 'protective'.

THERE IS NO SUCH THING AS A NEGATIVE ATTITUDE

Ireland is a politically divided island where preconscious attitudes towards different cultural and religious groups have led to centuries of hatred and violence. These attitudes fuel feelings of mistrust, insecurity and fear between the different groups. Such feelings arise from an even deeper source, which is the lack of valuing of the differences between the groups, and, even more so, the lack of acceptance and celebration of their common humanity. Whatever the cause that led to the loss of a sense of shared humanity, the solution must surely lie in a rediscovery of the wonder of being human and respect for and sharing of different religious, political and cultural heritages.

Examples of the *preconscious attitudes* that create the dividing line between the groups are:

- □ 'All Republicans are papists and agents of the devil.'
- □ 'All Unionists are murderous puppets of the British government.'

To call such attitudes 'irrational' or 'negative' is to miss the point of the very useful purpose they serve of keeping the two groups apart from each other and enabling both sides to put the blame for the division on each other. There is method in the seeming madness here because, until emotional changes of valuing and trusting each other come about, it is not safe to live with each other and, therefore, protective forces are needed. Again, with such attitudes towards each other, neither group has to take responsibility for change. The blaming of the other group maintains the protection of staying in separated camps and neither then has to risk the possibility of being rejected, humiliated and ridiculed by the other. Preconscious protective attitudes reflect mistrust between people and earlier experiences of abandonment, exploitation and diminution of one group by another. Until these deep emotional issues are resolved, people need as much protection from each other as possible, and the head is a great inventor of attitudes that protect the heart.

In the same way that divided communities develop protective attitudes, so too do conflictual couples. Many concerned people are astounded when women who have been physically, sexually and emotionally abused return to the abusive relationship, even though the offending partner has sought no help for his problems. The *rationalisations* often given are:

- 'He's not all bad.'
- 'He can't do without me.'
- 'The children need their father.'
- 'Where else can I go?'
- 'Things will change.'
- 'He'll mellow with age.'

Each of these conscious verbalisations – which are protective in nature – arises from the deeper source of *preconscious attitudes* such as:

- □ 'Avoidance of the difficult challenges and responsibilities in life is the best policy.'
- □ 'Things are the way they are and I can't do anything to change anything.'
- □ 'I'm getting what I deserve because I'm a bad person.'
- □ 'I'm useless and worthless and am unable to stand on my own two feet.'

Although these preconscious attitudes exert a powerful influence on the thinking, saying and doing of the women involved, these women are aware neither of the existence of the attitudes nor of their connection to conscious behaviours. This unawareness in itself protects the women from having to face up to vulnerabilities that, at this point, they have not got the emotional safety to tackle. To say such attitudes are 'irrational' or 'negative' serves only to further browbeat and humiliate the victims of the abuse. They need to be given credit for their masterly cognitive efforts to protect themselves from an even deeper hurt than that of the abuse of their partner – the pain of gross abandonment in childhood and the dread of experiencing again that total loss and isolation. At this point, they may not yet be able to see that their redemption lies in learning to cherish themselves, and so, in returning to their partners, they have at least some hope of being cherished. If throughout their lives their experience has been of neglect, abandonment, criticism and abuse, then they have no safety and no foundation from which to start their quest to find their own goodness, uniqueness, beauty, capability and lovability. They need the protection given by the kind of preconscious attitudes listed above.

In the first example, the attitude protects through avoidance of taking on the responsibility for separating out from the abusive partner. In the second example, which involves projection of all problems on to fate, the attitude offers the woman protection against owning what is happening to her and taking responsibility for change. The third and fourth examples involve introjection, where the woman regards herself as bad and worthless and deserving of the bad treatment; the protection in this attitude is that 'if I am so useless, how could anyone expect me to take on the threatening responsibility of separating out from an abusive partner?'

In workplaces you sometimes witness employees being exploited and abused by their employers. If you suggest to these employees that they confront their bosses and request respect and justice, they may respond with such *protective excuses* as:

- ☐ 'She has a lot on her plate at the moment running the business, family, children and so on.'
- ☐ 'He does have his good points.'
- ☐ 'I need this job.'
- ☐ 'I'm sure she doesn't mean it.'
- ☐ 'This is not a good time to talk to him.'

These statements on the conscious level protect against the confrontation which is too threatening to self-esteem to take on at this juncture. The *hidden (preconscious) protective attitudes* that lie at the roots of such statements may be:

- ☐ 'I should be perfectly competent in everything I do.'
- ☐ 'Being dependent on others is absolutely necessary in this life.'
- ☐ 'It is weakness to show vulnerability.'

These preconscious attitudes offer the employees who hold them a way out of having to confront, a way out that is needed until they are ready for openness. The first attitude involves introjection of demands to be perfect which not only protects marvellously against failure but also provides a good reason for not confronting unreasonable behaviour: 'After all, if my boss finds me wanting, it must be because I'm not perfect and it means I need to try harder.' I have worked with employees who will work up to twelve or fourteen hours a day in order to avoid failure and criticism and to please employers. Their perfectionist attitude protects them from having to look at their own extreme behaviours. It is a strong deterrent against putting the kind of responsibility on to the employer which would mean risking criticism and ridicule. It acts as a spur to greater efforts to please the employer and thereby reduces the possibility of hurt and rejection.

The second example of the kind of preconscious attitude an exploited employee might hold involves projection and cleverly blocks any attempts to threaten the source of dependence. The third example illustrates an ingenious use of introjection. In living according to the attitude that it is weakness to show vulnerability, the person protects herself from the possibility of rejection by never showing anger, frustration, hurt or resentment.

If you have a deep emotional sense of your own value and worth and your consequent right to be respected and valued, then you will not accept abuse from any quarter. You will firmly, calmly and respectfully assert your rights and when verbal confrontation does not gain you an appropriate response, you will take strong, firm and fair action. However, not too many of us have that inner safety to be able to confront in such a constructive way. While we are still struggling with old emotional hurts, we need protection against the possibility of repetitions of such experiences.

The preconscious attitudes which we have been discussing are creative and protective. They need to be valued and accepted as necessary in the person's life until safety is created. Then hidden conflicts can be revealed and the process of healing set in motion.

PROTECTIVE ATTITUDES RATHER THAN NEGATIVE ATTITUDES

If, as I suggest, you view so-called negative or irrational attitudes as, instead, protective, you are now honouring your psyche as caring for you, as constantly being active to protect you from further hurts and blocks to your development, and as attempting to lead you further down the road to self-actualisation. As with protective thoughts and feelings, there is a second function to protective attitudes – the function of alerting you to threats to your well-being, and to the changes that are needed to avert such threats. But, unless you have internal safety, you will not be able to respond to the alerting function of your attitudes and will instead respond to their protective message. In order to highlight these protective and alerting functions, I will take twelve examples of common preconscious attitudes and show for each one the threats to well-being that are implied and the healing that is needed.

- □ 'Everybody should like and love me.'
- □ 'I should be perfectly competent in everything I do.'
- □ 'People are inherently bad and should be punished for their evil nature.'
- □ 'Everything should go well for me in life and it is a catastrophe when it doesn't.'
- □ 'Life is determined by forces outside ourselves.'
- □ 'Avoidance of the difficult challenges and responsibilities in life is the best policy.'
- □ 'Being dependent on others is basic to all living.'
- □ 'I'm the way I am because of my past, and nothing can change that.'
- □ 'My life is determined totally by my genetic make-up.'
- □ 'I should always help others when they become distressed and upset.'

- ☐ 'People are only out for themselves.'
- ☐ 'People who show vulnerability are weak.'

'Everybody should like and love me.'
(Alerting message: 'I must like and love myself and be emotionally independent of others.')

This attitude involves projection, whereby you put all the responsibility for your happiness on to others and thereby protectively absolve yourself of all responsibility for your own feelings of unhappiness. You can now conveniently blame others for your 'down' days. In blaming others, you further protect yourself by not having to look at yourself at all. To do that would mean having to face your abandonment and rejection of yourself and the painful abandonment experiences of childhood that led you to view yourself in such a protective way. Notice also that the attitude involves no 'I' message, which means that you do not have to take any risk in requesting the love and affection you crave. This is resourceful because to ask for affection means risking rejection.

If you were secure within yourself and independent of others, your attitude would then be open rather than protective. Only then could you feel that it is desirable to be loved and accepted by others but it is not essential. Attitudes reflect your emotional state – this is what infuses them with power and determines whether they are protective or open.

Generally speaking, the healing implied in the protective attitude is psychodiametrically opposed to its explicit message. For example, the healing message in 'everybody should love me' is 'I must like and love myself'. The strong implicit message in this attitude is 'do precisely for yourself what you need others to do for you'. It is vital, however, that you do not start that journey until the risks involved for you have been lessened.

'I should be perfectly competent in everything I do.'
(Alerting message: 'Mistakes and failures are no index of my worth as a person.')

This example of a preconscious protective attitude arises from the internalisation of unrealistic demands of parents, teachers and other significant adults in your life, an internalisation which occurred as a protection against the wrath you feared would occur should you not meet their expectations. Pat yourself on the back for the ways you found to protect yourself from being further hurt and rejected. The message to others is very clear here: 'If I do everything right, will you accept and love me?' Perfectionist attitudes fuel the fire of compulsive perfectionist behaviours. The following poem reflects this protective cycle:

Perfectionist

You must know him
if not then her

Cleaning cleaning
never ending
running running
not moving
ever smiling
heart breaking

Doing everything
achieving nothing

Going everywhere
getting nowhere
endless racing

mindless pacing
things in place
love displaced

Perfection aim
remaining same

Again, emotional dependence on others has led to the creation of a protective attitude, and only when that emotional vulnerability is resolved will the person preconsciously dissolve this protective attitude. The healing necessary is implicit in the alerting message: 'Mistakes and failures are no index of my worth.' This open attitude will evolve only when an unconditional love of yourself has been established. If protective preconscious attitudes defend you from hurt, open attitudes reflect and reinforce your emotional maturity.

'People are inherently bad and should be punished for their evil nature.'
(Alerting message: 'People are inherently good and deserve to be loved and valued.')

The protection in this example becomes clear when you consider the implicit alerting message in the attitude. To see others as deserving love would mean taking major emotional risks of expressing affection and respect. How clever is the protection in seeing others as bad since no risk in reaching out to others is now required! The greater the emotional threat for you in expressing love to another, the more extreme the protective attitude has to be. By seeing others as 'bad', you can justify avoidance of any contact and, if contact does occur, you employ a further protective strategy of seeing people as only being worthy of punishment.

Obviously there are great dangers in this protective attitude. The attitude comes from the fact that the 'bad' things done to you at an earlier time were extreme and frequent, and so your need for protection against a recurrence is very great. Unfortunately, sometimes the 'evil' perpetrated on yourself is projected on to others through the very means that were used on you – violence, sexual abuse, rages, destruction of property, alcohol abuse, drug abuse. The aim is not to hurt others but to protect yourself. Nevertheless, the people who are at the receiving end of such protective but abusive responses need and deserve protection in return. In order to achieve this, society often imprisons the person employing such protective responses (and rightly so), but it offers little or nothing for the healing of the psychological hurts underlying the socially unacceptable behaviours. The obligation to protect others from these emotionally vulnerable and socially dangerous individuals is being met to some degree. However, sufficient recognition is not given to the fact that offenders themselves need protection and, above all else, a safe emotional environment, wherein their very damaged human spirits may begin to heal.

'Everything should go well for me in life and it is a catastrophe when it doesn't.'
(Alerting message: 'Take responsibility for your own life and see ups and downs as part of the positive process of learning.')

Very often this kind of protective attitude develops from overprotection in childhood, wherein all your needs were met with little or no effort required on your part. The unfortunate result of this child-rearing pattern is that you develop no sense of your vast capability to look after yourself. On the contrary, you emerge from childhood with a sense of helplessness, which is a major threat to your self-esteem. In order to guard against this emotional vulnerability, you resourcefully create the protective preconscious attitude which provides the rationalisation for avoidance of the risks involved in becoming more self-reliant. It is useless to condemn those who hold this protective attitude as 'irresponsible', 'lazy', 'no good', 'spoilt' since such responses only further diminish their already poor sense of self. These people have been disabled by overprotection, and they need the emotional safety of tolerance of their protective attitude and avoidance behaviours until the healing process is in motion and they become able.

'Life is determined by forces outside ourselves.'
(Alerting message: 'I can take charge of my own life.')

This attitude involves projection of responsibility for your life on to outside forces. The typical emotional history leading to this protective attitude is the dominating, controlling, critical and 'I know what's best for you' kind of parenting and teaching. It is very risky for children who experience such homes and schools to hold any opinions, or act in ways that are different from those of the adults who so control them. To do so would mean risking further experiences of emotional abandonment. The clever way out of this dilemma is never to exert any control over your own life, but to let forces outside you (parents, teachers, organisations, 'society', the church) take all the responsibility. In this way you eliminate risk-taking and threats to your self-esteem. These strong protectors are needed until you gain the safety to recognise your uniqueness and personal resources, and are strong enough to become separate from the control of others.

'Avoidance of the difficult challenges and responsibilities in life is the best policy.'
(Alerting message: 'Acceptance and active confrontation of the difficult challenges and responsibilities in life is the best policy.')

Avoidance and passivity are common protective responses when you do not have the emotional safety to be active, experimental, creative and confrontational in your living. Emotional unsafety is created when open behaviour in childhood is responded to with criticism, ridicule, scoldings, 'put down' messages, withdrawal of love, or physical violence. Because of the childhood history underlying the attitude, it is now vital not to condemn the adult who has expediently retreated into passivity and avoidance as the surest means of reducing the possibility of being hurt in this world. For such people, being actively assertive about their own needs and the needs of others can begin to occur only when such movement is greeted with encouragement, praise and admiration, and when they have discovered a sense of the wonder of their own being and their right to be different and active in this world.

'Being dependent on others is basic to all living.'
(Alerting message: 'Being dependent on myself and independent of others is the essential basis of self-actualisation.')

We are typically reared on a diet of dependence. Neither parents nor teachers rear children to be non-conformist and independent. Because of their own dependencies, adults often live their lives through children, possessing and controlling them in order to protect themselves from any risk of judgment or ridicule for being a 'bad' parent or teacher. In order to protect themselves from rejection, children intuitively learn that the safest policy is to be dependent and to give whatever is needed to significant adults in their lives to ensure approval, acceptance and love. For children to be separate and independent of approval from others would mean risking their prime need to be loved, recognised and valued.

Dependence, then, is a wise preconscious protective attitude born out of a history that taught you conditional love. Once you conformed to the conditions for approval – be good, be perfect, be clever, be quiet – you gained the recognition you needed, but at the terrible expense of your own unique development as a person. People who are dependent live according to the lives and needs of others, and are emotionally blocked from journeying down the road of self-actualisation, non-conformity and independence. The removal of conditionality from homes, classrooms, workplaces, churches and other social and political institutions is a major prerequisite for the development of the emotional safety that is needed before people can act on the alerting message of this protective attitude: 'Being dependent on yourself and independent of others is the essential basis of self-actualisation.'

'I'm the way I am because of my past, and nothing can change that.'
(Alerting message: 'My past has certainly greatly influenced the way I am in life today but I have immense resources to change those influences.')

Blaming the past is a common attitude involving projection. If you feel unsafe and have no resources or support for change – either from within yourself or from others – then it is a sensible projection. By blaming your vulnerability on your distant past, you protect yourself from all the risks that are involved in taking on the responsibility for the healing of your past hurts. It is important to appreciate how necessary it was for you to protect yourself in the unsafe world in which you were reared, but do also begin to seek out safe people and places that will provide the fertile ground for the healing and growth you so richly deserve.

'My life is determined totally by my genetic make-up.'
(Alerting message: 'I have vast physical, psychological and social resources to take charge of my own life.')

This attitude is similar to previous examples where life is seen as being determined by history or forces external to oneself. Basically the protection involves projecting all responsibility for yourself and your actions on to your genetic make-up. Once again, with this protection you effectively disown your vulnerability and absolve yourself from any responsibility for change. Such a protective projection suggests that in your childhood years nobody took responsibility for loving and caring for you and nobody modelled any responsible caring of themselves. To face the sad reality that your parents neglected you, and also failed to take responsibility for their own care, is a difficult thing to do if you do not yet possess the inner security of feeling your worth and lovability. Your protection is necessary until you find safety but it is important that you seek it out. There are people who do care and will recognise, love and value you.

'I should always help others when they become distressed and upset.'
(Alerting message: 'I need to be there for myself and be there in a freely chosen supportive way for others when they request help.')

There are people who have learnt to find recognition in the world through always being there when others are in distress. It is amazing how such individuals seem to find so many distressed people: they are like bees to honey. If you hold this attitude, it is of no help for others to tell you that it is silly and irrational, and serves only to exhaust you. The attitude has the clever and definite purpose of trying to meet your need to be wanted and of avoiding the much more threatening task of resolving your own hidden dependence. It is the lesser of two evils to be involved with other people's problems rather than your own.

The challenge of the attitude's alerting message – to be there for yourself – will be very threatening to you if, when growing up, you were told that 'you ought to be always there for others' and that 'to think about yourself is only selfish' or if you were given the conditional message by a parent that 'if you constantly meet my needs, you will be loved by me'. Many women and some men have developed this protective attitude which fuels a ceaseless caring for others. But until it is safe for them to say 'no' to demands made on them and 'yes' to caring for self, it is necessary for them to maintain this protective attitude.

'People are only out for themselves.'
(Alerting message: 'I need to watch out for myself.')

This attitude provides strong protection against the risks involved in reaching out to others. Many of your needs – emotional, social, sexual, intellectual, recreational, material – are met in relationships but, if your childhood experience was that 'no one was truly there for you', then it will be too risky to continue reaching out to others. The preconscious attitude that others are only out for themselves eliminates the risk of re-experiencing the pain and trauma of a neutral or actively punishing response to an expressed need.

People who hold such an attitude are very often misperceived as being independent, but it is a pseudo-independence. The hidden issue is that you are scared of asking anything of another in case your request (and thereby yourself) will be rejected. The fear is real and has cleverly led to the development of the protective attitude and the consequent avoidance behaviour. Once again, you need to appreciate the wisdom in your protection but it is important that you do not stay stuck in your protectiveness but rather seek safety and begin the healing process of making your needs known.

'People who show vulnerability are weak.'
(Alerting message: 'My weakness is my strength.')

Stereotyping has done much to create this protective attitude in men, and men have suffered as a consequence. For example, women tend to outlive men by an average of eight years and cardiovascular stress as a result of bottling up feelings is one of the main causes of death among men. Male children are often told, for example, that 'big boys don't cry' and 'big boys must be brave'. Some male children are also discouraged from expressing feelings of love and care by being told 'you're only a sissy' when they show such feelings. In the light of such experiences, the attitude that people who show vulnerability are weak makes a lot of sense, because it protects against the ridicule expected when vulnerability is shown. Men need liberation from this protective attitude because it has seriously blocked their emotional development. However, men will not join a liberation movement until it is somehow clearly demonstrated that it is safe to do so. For men to view weakness as strength is a long way down the road of personal development. Women, on the other hand, because it is safer for them to show vulnerability, are in a better position to act on the alerting message 'my weakness is my strength' and take whatever action is needed to resolve the vulnerability. Because men cannot even show their vulnerability, they are denied the strength that comes from exploring it.

IDENTIFYING YOUR PROTECTIVE ATTITUDES

Preconscious attitudes are those which are just below the surface of conscious behaviours (thinking, saying, doing, feeling) and are not too difficult to detect. You will identify more quickly those preconscious attitudes which are open in nature because these aid your self-actualisation process and pose no threat to you. An example of an open preconscious attitude is: 'People are inherently good but somehow life experiences cloud their good sense of themselves.' Such an open attitude may be easily detected from the conscious functioning of the individuals who hold it: they will be kind, considerate, fair, just, assertive (doing); they will express understanding of people's difficulties in living (saying); they will try not to judge people through their actions (thinking); and they will generally feel love and compassion for others (feeling).

Detecting protective attitudes from your conscious functioning, while harder than detecting open attitudes, can also be done. You can track the preconscious protective attitude from what you do, say and think. The higher your vulnerability, the more protectively reluctant you will be in pursuing this detection process.

Identifying protective attitudes from what you do

In detecting protective attitudes from your actions, it is useful to look for recurrent patterns of behaviour, such as having to do things always in a certain way, or never being late for an appointment, or never finishing a job you have started, or putting off things you need to do. If you have to do things compulsively in a certain way, the underlying preconscious attitude more than likely goes like this: 'I should be perfectly competent in everything I do.' If you have never been late for an appointment or missed a day at work (in spite, for example, of being ill), the hidden preconscious attitude might be: 'Everybody should like me and have high regard for me.' If you find your partner complaining 'you never finish anything you've started', the preconscious attitude fuelling this behavioural pattern may be: 'Avoidance of the difficult challenges and responsibilities in life is the best policy.' Putting things off until tomorrow most likely emerges from the same protective attitude.

Identifying protective attitudes from what you say

Your spoken words can be a powerful window into your preconscious attitudes and deeper hidden vulnerabilities. The idea here again is to track the attitude from what you typically or recurrently say. Some examples are:

- ☐ 'You won't catch me making a fool of myself.'
- ☐ 'I can't say "no" if someone asks for help.'
- ☐ 'People just don't care.'
- ☐ 'I'd never ask anybody for anything.'

The kinds of attitude which may underlie such statements are:

- ☐ 'Avoidance of the difficult challenges and responsibilities in life is the best policy.'
- ☐ 'I should always be there for others when they become distressed and hurt.'
- ☐ 'People are only out for themselves.'
- ☐ 'I should be perfectly competent in everything I do.'

Identifying protective attitudes from what you think

You can spend a lot of time in your head without being wholly aware of what has been preoccupying you. There is quite a difference between being in your head for analysis purposes and being there for worrying, obsessive and brooding purposes. The former can promote self-development, but the latter is a protective strategy that reflects hidden insecurities.

If you find yourself retreating into your head in a protective way, it can be valuable to pick up a pen and pad and spontaneously write out, without censoring, the thoughts going through your mind. Examples of such thoughts are:

- ☐ 'I hope people will like me at the dinner dance tonight.'
- ☐ 'I couldn't possibly stay home on my own.'
- ☐ 'I look awful.'
- ☐ 'I'll never change.'

Possible preconscious attitudes underlying such thought sequences are:

- ☐ 'Everybody should like and love me.'
- ☐ 'Being dependent on others is basic to all living.'
- ☐ 'Everything should go well for me in life and it is an absolute catastrophe when it doesn't.'
- ☐ 'I am the way I am because of my past, and nothing can change that.'

A good aid to your detective work is to keep a diary of the things you typically say and think when you are with others. From your diary, you will begin to spot recurrent patterns. When you have discovered the underlying protective attitude, then look for the alerting message in it and begin, when you feel ready, to move in the direction signposted by the attitude.

CHAPTER 5

THE POWER OF 'NEGATIVE' FEELINGS

THERE IS NO SUCH THING AS A NEGATIVE FEELING

Like thoughts and words, feelings too have been labelled as 'good' or 'bad' and 'positive' or 'negative'. Typically, such feelings as love, affection, warmth, confidence, optimism, joy, are seen as positive, and such feelings as hate, fear, guilt, anger, sadness, depression, loneliness, envy, jealousy are seen as negative. It is understandable why certain feelings have been given their 'bad' label because your outlook on self, others and life can be bleak, to say the least, when you are experiencing feelings like guilt, depression, fear or anger. There is some method in the madness of the 'negative' label since it provides the way out for not voicing those feelings which can be so threatening to your sense of self. But the negative labelling of these feelings blocks us from seeing their protective and deeper alerting functions:

- ☐ They are a creative response to perceived threats to self-esteem.
- ☐ They guard against the possibility of further experiences of hurt, abuse and humiliation.
- ☐ They are an attempt to alert you to the need for change.
- ☐ They provide the energy for the actions needed to bring about change.

If you are vulnerable, you are more likely to respond in the protective mode, whereas if you are high in self-esteem, you will possess the level of safety which enables you to go beyond protection and respond to the alerting function of the feelings.

PROTECTIVE FEELINGS RATHER THAN NEGATIVE FEELINGS

Many people feel bad about feeling bad. They are trapped in a cycle of hating the very feelings that are there to guide them towards maturity. But how, you may ask, can depression be a creative response to a crisis? The following example from my own life shows the power of so-called negative feelings.

I went into a monastery when I was eighteen years of age and left shortly before ordination. My parents were bitterly disappointed and really did not want to see me coming home. Nobody spoke to me on my homecoming, and on the third day I overheard my mother say to a neighbour 'it's such an embarrassment to have him around now'. I know now that my parents did not mean to abandon me in this time of major crisis in my life, but at the time I felt utterly alone and depressed. I left home the following day, sold a chalice I had been given and started on my journey of self-discovery. I was depressed for several years and prone to temper outbursts which, mercifully, only on the rare occasion ended in physical violence. At times I felt suicidal. I certainly did not see these feelings as creative, but now I see they were the impetus I needed to move out of home and away from a return to dependence on my family. Not only that, my depressive feelings afforded me protection against further hurt and abandonment as I avoided creating new relationships. Furthermore, my depression was attempting to wake me up to a deeper abandonment problem, which was my own hate and rejection of myself. Finally, though this was many years later, my feelings gave me the energy to heal my relationship with myself, my parents, others and the world.

Apart from depression, I had managed to manufacture a whole range of other protective feelings such as anger, resentment and social anxiety. These feelings further protected me from having to face up to myself (which I was not able to do at the time because the necessary supportive environment was not there) by putting the focus on others (anger and resentment) and by prompting me to avoid relationships (social anxiety).

I recall one client telling me how much she hated her two children, her husband and, most of all, herself. Many people's response to such a confession would be: 'How could any mother hate her children?'; 'Just what kind of a woman is she?' Such judgments would serve only to confirm this woman's worst fears about herself – that she is worthy only of being despised and rejected. My response to her confession surprised her. I told her compassionately that I really could understand why she hated her children, her husband and herself. I gently led her to see that her hate of others creatively protected her against and prepared her for what she felt would inevitably come about – that they would see how worthless she was, just as she saw herself. I also led her to see that in not showing love feelings to her children or her husband (or indeed, to anybody) she cleverly protected herself from a repeat of her own abandonment experiences in childhood by her parents. Most of all, in hating herself she had found virtually the ultimate protection, because if she hated herself she could not expect anyone else to love her, and she now had the rationale (subconscious) for not taking any emotional risks in relationships. Sadly, she had developed no friendships throughout her life and remained lonely and isolated, just as she had been as a child. Unfortunately, if her own children were disobedient she could be very violent towards them. Violence can never be justified, but the earthquake proportion of the response is the psyche's attempt to draw attention to very severe neglect of self, and in this case, of children also. Its whole purpose is not to hurt but to gain control and enforce loyalty. For this woman, the children's disobedience was, subconsciously, perceived as their abandonment and lack of love of her. All the feelings of hate my client experienced were:

- a creative protection of her in that they served to reduce feared further experiences of abandonment
- a loud signal to her of the unresolved abandonment of her childhood and her own ongoing rejection of herself
- a source of energy for her to take the actions needed to heal her deep and intense hurt.

Psychologically, all her feelings of hate and consequent neglectful actions towards her children, spouse and others were right, but socially they were having dire consequences for her children's welfare and her marriage. Unless the psychological rightness of protective feelings and behaviours is recognised, there is little chance that the person will be able to take on the social responsibility of healing her relationships with others. It was primarily through the emotional acceptance of herself that this woman managed to heal, eventually, the relationships with her children and, to some extent, with her husband. The reason her marital relationship continued to be problematic was that her partner refused to come for help for his own considerable vulnerability and remained largely helpless and dependent on her.

IDENTIFYING AND UNDERSTANDING PROTECTIVE FEELINGS

The protective feelings we most often experience are:

- fear
- depression
- guilt
- anger
- resentment
- frustration
- dissatisfaction
- grief
- jealousy.

As you have seen, these feelings are not 'negative' or 'undesirable' or 'bad' because they both protect you and alert you to the underlying conflict that needs to be healed. The frequency, intensity and duration of these protective feelings are determined by your level of insecurity and the depth of your unresolved childhood conflicts. Protective feelings are necessarily uncomfortable because they are an attempt to wake you up to the need to seek support and help so you may resolve your hidden insecurities.

Fear is protective

Fear is the most common feeling of all and can attach itself to so many objects: a person, a thing, the future, the past, God, evil and so on. Fear of failure is common to most people; it manifests itself, for example, in fear of examinations, fear of interviews, fear of making a date with someone, fear of being late, fear of public speaking, and fear of saying or doing the wrong thing in social or work situations. Fear of failure is strongly connected with not wanting to 'make a fool of yourself' or 'let yourself down in front of others' or 'make a laughing stock of yourself'. It is even more strongly connected to the need to be liked, accepted, valued and loved by others; any threat of failure is seen as a threat to this acceptance. This connection was made in childhood when failure became associated with feelings of hurt, humiliation and rejection. We learned a bitter lesson: in order to be loved and accepted we had better not fail.

How then does fear of failure perform the functions of alerting and protecting us? Let us take the example of a manager of a large company who has been requested to present a management package for the more effective running of the company. The manager feels panicky at the prospect, even though he has the information needed at his fingertips. He finds that his sleep is interrupted and he is dreading the day of the presentation. He experiences nausea, heart palpitations and excessive perspiration at the thought of the presentation. In spite of all this, his fear is creative and purposeful. It is alerting him to the fact that:

- He is dependent on success and on others' opinions of his performance.
- He lacks confidence in his own wondrous abilities.
- He is confusing confidence with competence.
- The focus of his unresolved childhood problems lies in the constant attempts to please his parents.

His fear is protective in that:

- It leads to compensatory or avoidance behaviours.
- It prepares him for the prospect of failure and provides the rationalisation that 'I knew I'd make a mess of it'.

The fear can provide him with the energy to become self-reliant and independent of success and of others' good opinion of him provided that the emotional safety is there in him to do so.

The confusion of confidence and competence by many people has been mentioned already. Confidence is knowing that you have limitless capability to become competent at anything to which you set your mind. Most people lack confidence in themselves and fear of failure serves to alert us to this serious self-esteem problem which needs to be resolved.

I have noted above that fear of failure is protective because it leads to compensatory and avoidance behaviours. In compensation you protect yourself by working very hard and for long hours so you get it so right you could not possibly fail or make a mistake. Avoidance is an equally effective protective strategy because by making no effort or taking no risk (in the example above, the manager perhaps gets physically ill on the day of the presentation or has a minor car accident) you cannot possibly fail.

A further protective strategy arising from fear of failure is to predict disaster: 'I know it will go all wrong.' The prediction has the purpose of reducing other people's expectations of you; should failure occur it provides the justification for it ('I knew it would happen') and dilutes the feelings of hurt and humiliation that may arise. This strategy is typical of students whose sense of worth is tied up with high academic performance. These students, who so much want to get As, will often proclaim 'I'll be lucky if I pass'.

A common fear in couple relationships is the fear of losing your partner. This fear can lead to either possessive, dominating and controlling behaviours (in order to enforce loyalty) or eagerness to please, overindulgence of your partner and passivity (in order to make yourself indispensable). This fear alerts you to:

☐ your dependence on your partner
☐ your insecurity and low level of self-reliance and self-regard
☐ your unresolved childhood conflicts and your non-separation from your parents.

Your fear protects you by:

- reducing or eliminating repetitions of rejection experienced in childhood
- prompting the protective behaviours of either aggression or passivity
- putting the focus on your partner and taking it off yourself.

The fear provides the energy (when you are ready) to resolve your inner conflicts and become independent in your relationship with your partner and your parents.

Depression is protective

Many of the people who come to me for help suffer from deep feelings of depression, despair and hopelessness. How is this depression protective? The primary protective function of depression is to prompt a series of internal and external actions that reduce threats to your self-esteem and the possibility of failure and rejection by others. Take the example of depression following the birth of a child, which is not uncommon and is all too often put down to a biological reaction. My experience of women suffering postnatal depression is that its source is an underlying self-esteem problem which is in danger of being exposed following the birth of the baby. Because these women have hidden insecurities, because they fear failure and lack confidence in their ability to cope with the enormous responsibilities of child-rearing, depression arises in order to protect against these threats to their need to be valued and recognised. Postnatal depression in a mother may result in the following:

- withdrawal from her baby (protection: 'I can't fail if no effort is made on my part.')

- withdrawal from spouse and others (protection: 'Maybe they'll have sympathy for me and take over the responsibilities that so threaten me.')
- introjection, for example, 'I'm useless' (protection: 'Nobody could expect anything of me when I'm this bad.')
- rationalisation, for example, 'It must be a biochemical problem' or 'I'm just so exhausted' (protection: 'The problem is beyond my control and, so, I can't be held responsible.')
- regression into bouts of helplessness and uncontrollable crying (protection: 'If I'm helpless like a child, then somebody will take care of me and not demand anything of me.')

The postnatal depression is the psyche's attempt to alert the mother to unresolved conflicts from her own childhood but, until the safety is there for her to respond to the alerting function of her depression, she will necessarily respond in the protective mode.

When depression follows a major life event (such as the birth of a child, getting married, leaving home, changing job) or a major personal or interpersonal crisis (such as examination failure, loss of job, demotion, death of a loved one, breakdown of a long-term relationship) it is generally known as reactive depression. What is often not seen is that the depressive reaction to the life event is only the reflection of an underlying vulnerability that was already there, but is now in danger of being exposed and hence the need for the protective response. There are other types of depression that are not so easily traceable to a particular preceding event. These depressions tend to be labelled as endogenous or bipolar, and are sometimes seen as inherited.

I recall a young mother of one child who was told she had endogenous depression. This was described to her as a biological/

biochemical depression for which there is no known cause or cure and which requires lifelong drug treatment for some relief of the symptoms. She had received multiple electro-convulsive treatments which had given no relief from the depressive feeling. She was also on a high dosage of antidepressant medication and she had had several admissions to psychiatric hospital since the onset of the depression two years previously. Shortly before her first visit to me, she had attempted suicide. The reason she gave for the suicide attempt was that she saw no hope for the future given the prognosis: that she would experience this depression for the rest of her life and would have to stay on lifelong medication.

Because of such unsupportive and hopeless messages, I felt her suicide attempt made total sense. Why stay in a world that provides no safety and security for you? There was no obvious reason why this woman had become depressed. Nonetheless, I felt sure her depression had a deep protective meaning. At one stage I happened to ask her: 'When do these feelings mostly arise?' She answered, 'I could be combing my little girl's hair (aged three years at the time) and I would feel a well of sadness inside of me and think I'm going mad'. Now she had given me a window into her hidden conflict. When I asked her if, when she was a little child, her mother gently held and caressed her, the floodgates opened. What had happened was the lifting of repression of her underlying grief. Her metaphorical description was so accurate: 'I felt a well of sadness inside me.' Repression is the protective mechanism that children cleverly use to bury traumatic experiences that are too painful and threatening to look at on a daily basis. There is nothing more traumatic than rejection by a parent, but this is what my client had experienced as a very young child. The mother–child relationship with her daughter in the present time had triggered the deeply repressed rejection experience of childhood.

I believe that her psyche recognised the need for her to face up to and resolve this rejection experience, not only so that she could become more fulfilled within herself, but also so that she could now give her own child what she had not been given when she was a child. I also believe that the repression of the early rejection would not have lifted unless she had been ready to work on her problems. It was unfortunate that she did not get the understanding and emotional safety needed when the depression first occurred, but in the security of her relationship with me she did resolve her feelings of rejection by her mother and her consequent self-esteem problems. In moving from the very strong protective strategy of repression to the less strong protective strategy of depression, it seemed to me she had shown some readiness for healing. Nonetheless, before and during the process of healing the protective power of depression was needed. The further she progressed down the road of healing the extreme hurts she had experienced as a child and had unwittingly perpetuated as an adult, the more the depressive feelings began to abate and be replaced with joy and love of self, others and life.

Guilt is protective

All of us, at one time or another, have felt the pangs of guilt in our stomachs but perhaps without realising the wisdom and protective power of its presence. How is guilt protective? For example, if you are tempted to steal an object and you have a strong value that stealing is wrong, then guilt arises so that you will engage in actions to either resist the temptation or prevent possible discovery if you happen to give in to the temptation.

I have met many people who experience guilt because of obligations to parents. More often than not, the parents involved are strong and healthy but, somehow, their adult children feel this tremendous sense of obligation to phone and visit regularly, as if their parents would die without such contact. These people will expose themselves, their marriages and even their own children to considerable inconvenience and discomfort in order to fulfil what they see as their obligations to parents. I have worked with clients, both male and female, who go home to parents without fail every weekend of their lives. How is such guilt protective when it involves such neglect of their own development and independence? The answer lies in these people's deep fear of rejection by their parents. For them, it is the lesser of two evils to disrupt their own lives and even those of others important to them, rather than risk a repeat of the rejection they suffered from their parents in childhood. The guilt drives them into thoughts and actions that ensure that their obligations to parents are met and thereby reduces the possibility of hurt and rejection. How wise then the guilt is!

The other clever function of the guilt is that through the intense, uncomfortable feeling it is attempting to wake them up to the continuation of emotional dependence on their parents and to a deeper conflict, which is the rejection and neglect of themselves. The guilt here is much more about awakening to neglect of themselves rather than neglect of their parents. After all, the parents in question were not in ill-health. (Clearly, if parents become disabled, then it is the responsibility of all family members to share out the caring tasks.) Charity and love always begin at home and when such personal caring is not present then guilt arises to wake us up to this neglect. The people who feel guilt about parents or some other significant relative need the guilt to protect them from feared repetition of rejection and, until they have resolved their emotional dependence, the guilt will necessarily persist. In turn their dependence problems will truly be resolved only when the deeper message of this type of guilt is listened to and they begin to discover their own value and worth independent of parents and all others.

Many young people experience guilt if they contravene the values and morals of their parents. The guilt arises to prompt actions that will avoid discovery of the behaviour they fear will be met by harsh rejection by parents or religious leaders. The guilt here also has an alerting function, in that it seeks to push young people to question whether inherited ways are right for them and are caring and respectful of them as persons. If the answer to these questions is no, as it can frequently be, then the establishment of their independence from parents and church on these issues becomes an expedient task. The hope is that parents and others will respect and support this individualising process. The more dependent the young person is on parents, the more difficult this liberating process will be.

Anger is protective

The purpose of anger is to alert you to threats to your self-esteem and to protect you from such onslaughts. Anger provides energy to fuel either protective action or the action needed for change. If you are vulnerable, rather than responding to the alerting function of your anger, you will tend to respond protectively. The two major ways of dealing protectively with anger are aggression at one extreme, and passivity at the other. For example, if a partner, colleague or friend tells you what to do, say and wear, you may feel a tide of anger well up. If you are dependent on the person attempting to control you, you may protect yourself by suppressing your anger, thereby avoiding possible rejection for asserting your right to say, do and wear what you choose. On the other hand, you may protect yourself by projecting your anger on to the person who is being dominating with an aggressive statement such as 'you can't let people alone can you?' or 'you think you know everything'. Such projection protects you by putting the focus on the other person and taking it away from you. Of course, the projection is also an attempt to force the other person into not being so critical of you. Unfortunately, even though you do not intend it, your blaming of the other person may result in him feeling hurt, and he either attacks back or withdraws from you in order to reduce your onslaught. Aggression breeds either aggression or passivity; in neither case does it provide the supportive environment necessary for the two people involved – both of whom are vulnerable – to reach out for real personal and interpersonal change. Because aggression creates unsafety, both parties necessarily remain tied to their protective strategies. The second function of anger in the present example is to alert you to the need to assert your own independence and individuality, and to give you the energy to do so in a way that does not hurt or put down the person who is dominating you: 'I want to be seen as a person who can make decisions for myself.'

The anger is there for your emancipation, not to control the other. However, because we are so vulnerable to criticism and rejection we often do not listen to our anger in this way, but tend instead to deny, suppress, dilute or project the feeling – all in an attempt to reduce further experiences of hurt and humiliation. Until you have emotional safety, you need these protective strategies. Many of my clients have strong feelings of anger towards parents or spouses whom they feel dominated, controlled, manipulated and hurt them. Such blaming is expedient until these clients are ready to own their own lives and take on the responsibility of resolving their dependence on others. Through the gentlest of processes, I try to provide the emotional safety where they can see how they had needed to blame others in order to protect themselves from further hurt but how now, as they grow in love and respect for themselves, they can begin to let go of these protective strategies.

Resentment is protective

Resentment is akin to anger but, rather than being expressed in aggression, it more typically leads to the protective actions of withdrawal, sulking, non-co-operation and gossip. The first three protective reactions involve no risk-taking on your part, but they do push the person who has offended you to chase after you and try to find out what is bothering you. Naturally, if the person who has offended you is equally vulnerable, then he is unlikely to take this risk and so both of you stay stuck in your protective mode and no resolution is attained. Even greater protection is provided by gossip where you totally mask your feelings of resentment from the people involved but, behind their back, gossip about their faults.

You may find yourself feeling resentful if, for example, somebody offers you advice without your requesting it. The resentment arises because the unsolicited advice is a threat to your self-esteem and its function is to give you the energy to assert yourself: 'I do not find it helpful when you give me advice without my asking for it.' However, if your self-esteem is low, you will find it difficult to engage in such clear communication. Instead you may say nothing, nod your head in pseudo- agreement, change the subject, or excuse yourself and move away – all clever protective strategies to reduce the possibility of further hurt from ill-given advice and attempts to control and dominate you. However, these protective strategies maintain your underlying vulnerability and the deeper message of the resentment is to seek the safety you need in order to resolve your vulnerability.

If your needs are not being considered, resentment will wisely arise to remind you that you are responsible for your own needs and that it is up to you to express them – whether to partners, friends, work colleagues, neighbours or others. It is not for others to read your mind, but when you fear rejection or ridicule that is precisely the protective strategy you are likely to employ. 'If I don't ask, then I can't be refused' is the protective ploy here. You also transfer all the responsibility to recognise your needs on to the other and so no risk-taking is needed on your part. It would not be wise for the significant people in your life to collude with this protective strategy, because their collusion serves only to maintain your, and indeed their, vulnerability.

Resentment is common in workplaces where nepotism, unfair practices, destructive criticism and unfair expectations threaten the self-esteem of employees. Vulnerability may prevent you from using the energy in the feeling of resentment to assert your worth and value as a person in such an organisation, and to voice your just needs to be respected, consulted, positively criticised and given a tolerable amount of responsibility. Vulnerability may result in the resentment being expressed in protective reactions of compensation (working even harder and for longer hours in order to please and prevent conflict) or avoidance (absenteeism, psychosomatic complaints such as headaches, colds, flu, back-pain) or minimal effort (the less you do, the less risk of hostility). Such protective strategies are necessary until you come to the point where you have sufficient personal security to confront the unfair and troubling situation.

Frustration is protective

When your needs are blocked, you feel frustrated. You may, for example, feel frustrated if your sexual needs are not being met. The feeling is there to alert you to do something about resolving the block. If, however, you are vulnerable, you are unlikely to pay heed to your frustration in this way, but instead express it in protective action such as not talking about your sexual needs (no risk here), having an extramarital affair (avoidance tactic), using self-stimulation as a substitute (avoidance behaviour) or maybe just doing without (passivity).

Frustration also rears its head when things do not work out as you want, for example a do-it-yourself job that goes against you. In frustration you may let out a roar, thump the nearest object, throw up the job, persist until the bitter end or blame the person who asked you to do the job: 'you always give me an awkward job, don't you?' or 'this is just impossible' or 'I'm just sick of this'. These reactions protect in a number of ways:

- release of pent-up tension
- avoidance (no more attempts, no more failure)
- compensation ('If I stay at it until I get it right, I can't fail.')
- projection (you distract from your own difficulties)
- introjection ('How can you expect any more of me?').

If you have high self-esteem, you will use the frustration to discover what you need to do in the situation. This may include:

- doing the job more slowly
- accepting that it is too difficult and that you require some expert help
- taking time out and returning when you feel calmer and more in control
- requesting help from someone
- admitting that you did not really want to take on the task in the first place.

Dissatisfaction is protective

Job dissatisfaction is a common phenomenon but, regrettably, many people do not listen to and act on the feeling by taking the steps necessary to resolve the issues leading to the feeling. If you are low in self-esteem, then your dissatisfaction may be expressed in protective action such as illness. Job dissatisfaction, as mentioned earlier, is the strongest predictor of heart disease, much more so than a history of heart disease in the family, high blood pressure or high cholesterol levels. I have had clients who suffered heart attacks or brain strokes and were subsequently confined to wheelchairs and whose spouses told me they had never seen them happier! Not so surprising when you see that in being wheelchair-bound, no expectations, work or otherwise, could be made of them and so they had found a very effective protection against failure and worry. Inevitably, I found that such clients had deep fears of failure, had been absolute perfectionists in their jobs and had been highly sensitive to criticism. Their protective strategy was very necessary for them.

Dissatisfaction may also arise when, for example, you get poor service in a restaurant. Many people will not confront the poor service because they fear causing embarrassment (avoidance). But the person who strongly feels he is worthy of good service will pay heed to and act on the dissatisfied feeling by politely and firmly pointing out the shortcomings of the service to the service-provider, and requesting either compensation or improved service. How few of us do that is indicative of the widespread existence of insecurity among us.

The dissatisfaction is there to provide you with the energy to resolve the issue in question but, if you are vulnerable, you will use that energy instead to protect you from threats to your fundamental need to be loved, recognised and valued in this world.

Grief is protective

Grief is a feeling we are all likely to experience at some point in our lives. If, for example, we lose a parent or a close friend, grief creatively arises to alert us to the necessity to seek support, comfort, warmth and quiet during this time of loss. Again, as with other feelings, the person may act on the grief or may respond in a protective manner. Prolonged grief, for example, is a protective strategy against hidden vulnerabilities that are now in danger of being exposed following the experience of loss. A high percentage of widows and widowers die within a short time of their spouse's death, even though they have shown no signs of ill-health prior to the bereavement. Many of these spouses say things like 'I have no reason to go on now' or 'I want to be with her' or 'what's the point of it all now?' The hidden vulnerability is that they never really had possession of their own lives and the loss of the spouse has highlighted a lifetime of dependence on another. Because it is so difficult now for them to face up to taking care of themselves, to be independent and self-sufficient, protective strategies are need-ed to guard against the terrifying vulnerability that is there. Prolonged grief or early death are some such strategies. Prolonged grief is expressed in withdrawal from activities, neglect of personal welfare and the wish for death – all avoidance strategies that guard against failure and exposure of hidden massive doubts about self. Individuals who experience prolonged grief reactions are in need of the safety and support of psychotherapy. It helps when family, friends and others show belief in their ability to continue with their lives, express warmth and affection and gently encourage involvement in activities, and later on, new challenges.

People with a love of self, of others and of life will go through a period of grieving when someone dear is lost and that person will always remain an intimate part of their lives. But they will also move on with their own lives and refuse to live in the past.

Jealousy is protective

The functions of jealousy are to protect you from feared rejection or feared loss of a partner, lover or friend and, at a deeper level, to alert you to your own rejection and abandonment of yourself. Of course, if you are vulnerable, you will be unable to listen to the alerting message and will respond instead in a protective way. I recall the case of a young married man whose feelings of jealousy were so intense that he was catapulted into the extreme protective actions of:

- being very possessive
- checking up on his partner's movements, even to the point of following her
- checking her pockets and handbags to find evidence of unfaithfulness
- frequently phoning her on the pretext of wanting to make contact but really to check up on her
- questioning her on past affairs
- sulking when she spoke to another man when they were out socially
- accusing her of wanting to be with someone else or having secretly met a new lover.

All his unreasonable behaviours were protective mechanisms, designed not to hurt his partner but to enforce her loyalty to him. They were projections of his uncertainty about himself on to his partner and imagined or real rivals. As with many such men I have worked with, he was abandoned emotionally by his mother in his early years. That frightened, insecure, unloved child was still present in adulthood, and subconsciously was expecting a similar fate again and was desperately trying to hold on to his partner. Deep down he had no regard for himself and could not believe that his partner could really love him. None of the protestations of love by his partner was powerful enough to break through the wall of his own emotional conviction of his unlovability. His feelings of jealousy continued to protect him until he got the help he needed to heal the pain deep within him and eventually came to a place of love and acceptance of himself.

LEVELS OF PROTECTIVE FEELING

Feelings are the first and most powerful means of protecting and alerting you when you are vulnerable. The feelings discussed so far are those that you experience consciously but there are certain preconscious feelings that operate just below the surface of your conscious awareness. These feelings not only fuel your conscious feelings but are also the source of your protective thinking and actions. They will stay at the preconscious level until you are ready to face your hidden vulnerabilities. Examples of preconscious feelings are:

- insecurity
- suppressed anger
- lack of confidence
- distrust
- anxiety
- guilt
- dislike of self.

At an even deeper level again may be found the subconscious feelings which are the well-spring of all conscious and preconscious protective behaviours. The subconscious emotional protectors arise when the deepest longing of all human beings – the need for unconditional love – is not met and the person is left to cope with his experience of emotional abandonment. Depending on the extent and intensity of the abandonment experiences, people build up subconscious protective walls in order to reduce the occurrences of rejection. The most common subconscious protective feeling is fear of abandonment. Another subconscious emotional protector is repression from conscious awareness of unbearable rejection experiences – sexual abuse, physical violence, great hostility or passivity, physical neglect and extreme conditionality. All preconscious and conscious protectors stem from and strengthen the subconscious protectors.

The following story of a young man may clarify how protective feelings operate at the three levels: conscious, preconscious and subconscious. The young man was a teacher in his late twenties who was sent to me by his general medical practitioner. The presenting physical problems were high blood pressure and ulcerative colitis. His medical doctor suspected that the sources of his physical problem lay in an underlying high anxiety condition. My initial question was: 'What are the high blood pressure and ulcerative colitis saying about the emotional life of this teacher?' The answer to this question lay partially in what he daily felt, thought, said and did. Every day he was driven to carry out his responsibilities perfectly. When he awoke each morning he dreaded and worried about the day's work and would protectively think 'have I everything prepared?'; 'will I remember everything?'; 'will I be able to keep contol of my classes?' Often he would get physically sick before leaving for work. Any extracurricular activity that the school principal requested he would volunteer for in a flash, 'I'll do that', and he would do it perfectly. 'Better than anyone before' is how he described it to me. His conscious feeling protectors were:

- feeling of intense dedication to his teaching responsibilities
- feelings of worry and fear – these kept him alert to the threats to his self-esteem and drove him into the protective thoughts and actions described above
- eagerness to please – in order to be liked, valued and accepted.

Underlying these conscious feeling explanations for his high blood pressure and ulcerative colitis were preconscious feelings of serious insecurity and, arising from the latter, the protective attitudes of 'I should not fail', 'I should be perfect', 'everybody should like me'. He was not consciously aware of these deeper feelings since such awareness would be too threatening and could undermine the protective strategies he had in place to guard against failure and rejection. The psyche was wise to keep this information at a preconscious level.

A deeper subconscious explanation for the development of the protective preconscious feelings of insecurity eventually revealed itself. His subconscious problem was feelings of very low self-esteem and terror of abandonment. All his extreme perfectionist behaviours – of needing to be the best, of dreading and worrying, of long hours working – now made total sense: all were means of protecting his low self-esteem and guarding against any possibility of rejection by others. In his childhood, no matter how well he did in anything, whether academically, athletically, domestically, or otherwise, the response of both parents was 'you could have done better'. The condition for love and regard in this family was behavioural perfection – an unattainable expectation. But he was doing everything in his power to climb those impossible heights and at such a risk to his physical well-being. His case bears out my belief that a human being will risk everything, even life itself, in order to gain love and acceptance in this world. It was only as my unconditional love and acceptance of him began to be internalised by him that all the levels of his problem became consciously clear to him and the motivation and determination to heal these problems emerged. His was a journey of discovery of his worth and value independent of any behaviour and of separation from dependence on his parents and on others who had become substitute parents in his life.

It can be seen, therefore, that protective preconscious feelings of insecurity, unsureness and poor confidence spring from subconscious feelings of hate or dislike of self and, most of all, fear of abandonment. The subconscious emotional needs of human beings are to be loved, cherished, assured, accepted, valued, recognised and respected. Any threat to these needs results in the fear of abandonment, of not being loved, valued and cherished. Because conditional loving is part and parcel of the emotional experience of most young children, it is no wonder that most adults have some subconscious fear of not being loved and accepted. When you subconsciously doubt your lovability and capability and remain, like a child, dependent for approval on parents and others, then your psyche has to resort to a creative range of preconscious, conscious and physical means to protect you from further hurt and abandonment.

CHAPTER 6

THE POWER OF 'NEGATIVE' ACTION

THERE IS NO SUCH THING AS NEGATIVE ACTION

Just as thoughts have been categorised as positive or negative, so too actions have been labelled as 'good' or 'bad', 'rational' or 'irrational' and 'adaptive' or 'maladaptive'. People are given credit and seen as virtuous when they demonstrate 'good' actions, and are seen as 'troublesome', 'problematic', 'bad' and even 'evil' when they exhibit 'bad' actions. In the face of this tide of judgments, I want to assert that there is no such thing as negative action and that, like protective thinking, 'negative' action serves a powerful double function: the function of protection and the function of drawing attention to the need for resolution of underlying emotional conflicts.

'Negative' action is always right psychologically because of these protective and alerting functions. Nevertheless, it is understandable that protective actions are regarded as negative since they affect the lives of others in a negative way. Aggressive and dominating behaviour is typically labelled as 'negative' or 'maladaptive'. People often believe that its function is to control the other person but this is not so. The person who employs aggression as a means of getting needs met has deep emotional insecurities and the function of the aggression is to ensure the other's loyalty and so protect against rejection. The person who employs aggression has an inner emotional conviction of unworthiness and feels that the only way she can keep someone bound to her is through control. A further function of aggression is that all responsibility is projected away from you and on to the other person and the total focus is on the other – both of which protect you from having to look at your own vulnerability.

It is revealing to witness what happens when the protective tactic of aggression either fails to ward off rejection or the other person does not accept the projection. Very often the aggressive person will switch to another protective behaviour which is opposite in nature to the aggression, such as crying, threatening to hurt oneself, sulking or withdrawing. The tactic now is to get the other person to feel sorry for you and, should this happen, you have succeeded in protecting yourself from rejection. Furthermore, by now engaging in introjection ('I know I'm bad'; 'I'm awful to have shouted'; 'It won't happen again') you have found a means of not having to resolve the hidden emotional conflicts that led to your aggression in the first place: 'after all, if I'm such a "bad" person, how could I or anyone else expect anything of me?' Projection (for example, 'you'd better do what I tell you' or 'don't you dare disagree with me') is an obvious protective means to ensure that 'you will always be there for me', whereas introjection (for example, 'I know I am useless' or 'I never do anything right') more subtly protects by inviting the other person to take responsibility for you.

PROTECTIVE ACTION RATHER THAN NEGATIVE ACTION

So-called negative behaviours then serve the purpose of:

- protecting you from yourself (that is, from having to face up to unresolved emotional issues)

□ protecting you from others (that is, ensuring that childhood experiences of hurt, humiliation, trauma and rejection are not repeated).

These behaviours are not devised to hurt other people (even though this can often be the result, particularly with children) but to protect yourself from hurt. Protective action may be categorised under two main headings: undercontrol and overcontrol behaviours. A typical overcontrol protective behaviour is being extremely quiet, shy and withdrawn. Staying in the shadows protects you because you have to take no emotional risks; such protection is psychologically necessary for you because of underlying emotional vulnerability. This kind of protective behaviour does not upset the lives of others in any serious way and therefore it is not as socially inappropriate as undercontrol behaviour. Examples of undercontrol behaviour are temper tantrums, shouting, stealing and violence. Even though these undercontrol actions are just as psychologically necessary as overcontrol behaviours, they are, however, much more likely to be condemned and seen as grossly unacceptable – and rightly so! People cannot be allowed to protect themselves by means that make other people's lives difficult. However, little progress will be made in helping individuals who manifest under-control behavioural protectors if the psychological rightness of the behaviour is not seen alongside its problematic social effects. Compassion is vital; it enables you to see that the person is not being deliberately socially unacceptable but is using the best means of protection currently available to her.

I recall working with an adolescent girl who was stealing large sums of money at home, in school and in the homes of relations. She was caught regularly and was castigated severely by both parents and was sometimes even physically beaten by her father.

In spite of these punishing consequences, the stealing continued. The questions in my mind when she was brought to see me by her parents were: 'In what way is this girl's stealing psychologically right?' and 'What are the protective functions of the behaviour?' The social unacceptability of the stealing (undercontrol behaviour) was clear but this awareness on the girl's part (as well as on the part of her parents and other significant adults in her life) had not altered the behaviour in the slightest. Indeed, the stealing had become more extreme over time. I felt that unless the psychological rightness of the stealing was determined and recognised, then it was unlikely that the behaviour would change, no matter how strong the social deterrents. What I eventually discovered was that the stealing had begun when the girl was eight years of age (some nine years before) and had worsened over the years. What precipitated the stealing was the sudden death of her younger brother, whom both parents had spoilt. She herself was very fond of her brother but, sadly, following his sudden death, she was sent off to an aunt for three weeks. She did not see her brother's body nor did she attend the burial. When she returned home, no mention was made of the boy and she quickly picked up that his name was taboo. Both parents were in deep mourning and when I met them nine years later, neither of them had resolved their grief for the loss of their son. Not only did the girl have her brother stolen from her but also both parents became lost to her. They moved house quite soon after the death of the child and so she had the added loss of her friends and schoolmates.

This girl's undercontrol protective behaviour of stealing reflected the huge emotional losses she had experienced over the previous nine years and was a means of compensation. The protection was that the money could buy her friends, comforts, luxuries that in some small way compensated for the loss of her brother and, even more so, the loss of her parents' love and attention. The stealing also was a cry for help, an appeal for somebody to see the emotional desert that had been created in this family. Furthermore, the stealing was a projection outwards of her own need to be loved and it also offered the protection of not having to look at the deep feelings of rejection she had experienced earlier as a young child and continued to experience up to the present.

When I revealed to herself and subsequently to her parents how wise and necessary the stealing had been, and how the emotional issues within each of them as well as between them now needed to be resolved, all were very co-operative. No further incidences of stealing occurred – it had done its protective and alerting jobs well. The pity is that its purpose had not been recognised earlier since, unfortunately, the punishments meted out served only to deprive the girl further of the love and affection she so dearly needed.

TYPES OF PROTECTIVE ACTION

Undercontrol protective actions are more common among males, while overcontrol is more common among females. This is due to conditioning, where males are encouraged more towards aggressiveness and women more towards passivity. But the two types of behaviour are alike in that both act as means of protection and also serve as strong indicators of the need for emotional change. Because of their importance as signals for change, I have listed below some of the more common overcontrol and undercontrol protective behaviours. If you recognise any of these behaviours as occurring in your own life, try not to allow such signals to be flown in vain but instead acknowledge their message to you and see what changes you need to make. In reading through the examples keep in mind the following points:

- ☐ The behaviours are always psychologically right because they are adaptive strategies developed in response to childhood hurts and neglects.
- ☐ The behaviours serve the protective function of saving you from having to look at your own vulnerability and saving you from the possibility of others' rejection of you.
- ☐ Whether the behaviours involve a projection on to others or an introjection into self, they are subconscious mechanisms which attempt to get others to take responsibility for you.
- ☐ The behaviours are always indicators of the need for emotional change.
- ☐ The behaviours are not the problem; they are the signs of the hidden unresolved conflicts which are the real problem and they represent opportunities for change.
- ☐ The targets for change are the hidden emotional issues.

UNDERCONTROL PROTECTIVE BEHAVIOURS

☐ Being hostile towards others	☐ Being sarcastic
☐ Being quick-tempered	☐ Being destructive of own or others' property
☐ Being physically violent	
☐ Shouting, screaming	☐ Stealing
☐ Dominating and controlling	☐ Having temper tantrums
☐ Being cynical	☐ Blaming others for your own mistakes

Such undercontrol behaviours are seen as socially undesirable and those adults and children who engage in them are the people most often referred to health professionals. This is not surprising because their behaviours put other people's well-being at risk. However, the other side of the coin is that the person who shouts loudest is also the person who draws attention to the problem and is the most likely to get the help needed to face unresolved inner turmoil. I often tell parents and teachers that the child who is disruptive is very often the strongest member of a family in distress: not only does she draw attention to her own emotional plight, but she also highlights the even deeper problems of the parents and the family as a unit.

OVERCONTROL PROTECTIVE BEHAVIOURS

- Being shy, reserved and quiet
- Being passive
- Constantly pleasing others
- Having little concern for self
- Accepting of abuse from others
- Being timid and fearful
- Being non-assertive of own needs
- Turning a blind eye to abuse of others
- Avoiding confrontation
- Being a perfectionist
- Being obsessional
- Being compulsive

It is clear that overcontrol behaviours do not seriously interfere with the lives of others. It is therefore not surprising that people who display such protective actions are referred considerably less often to health professionals. Nonetheless, they need as much help as those children and adults who manifest undercontrol behaviours and are often at greater risk (physically, psychologically or socially) because they bottle up their inner conflicts to a far greater degree than their 'undercontrol' counterparts. If you do not express your inner frustrations, nobody else is going to risk confronting your unremitting neglect of yourself. Even if someone does confront you, you may very well find some other overcontrol action (for example, withdrawal) to protect you from such threatening openness and concern. This is not because you are ungrateful for expressed concern but because you may not yet be ready to trust or receive such warmth; you may fear letting in the message or the messenger in case they may be false and you would then wind up feeling neglected and abandoned once again.

INTERPERSONAL CONFLICT IS CREATIVE AND PROTECTIVE

It is clear that certain protective actions, because of their socially unacceptable nature, often lead to interpersonal conflict. Generally conflict is viewed as 'bad', 'something that shouldn't happen' and 'negative'. The response to it may be to bury your head in the sand and hope the situation will resolve itself, or to blame yourself or others or the world for it. All these responses are protectors against the hidden vulnerabilities from which the conflict is emerging. But such protective responses mean that the alerting function of the conflict, which points to underlying emotional issues, now goes unrecognised.

Conflict is always both protective and creative, as is illustrated in the following example of a couple in conflict. The husband controls and dominates his spouse by telling her constantly what to do, where to go, what to wear and how to be. For years she passively accepts his dominating behaviours. Interpersonal conflict arises only when the protective behaviours of either spouse cease to work. The breakdown in protection will happen if one of the spouses changes emotionally so that he or she is no longer willing to accept the other's dominance or passivity. In the present example conflict may arise when, for example, the female partner, because of some emotional change, is no longer willing to accept being controlled and ordered about by her partner. His protective behaviour now comes under threat and it may well be escalated in an attempt to bring his spouse back under his control so that she cannot leave or reject him. If she has got 'the bit between her teeth', she may stoutly resist his increased protective actions. This will threaten him even further and the conflict will continue to spiral. In his panic he may change his protective tactics to help-lessness, crying, not eating, threatening to hurt himself and so on. The conflictual behaviour of both persons serves the function of protection: his to reduce the possibility of rejection and also to avoid having to look at his own vulnerability; hers to hold on to her new-found sense of her own worth and value and also to remain determined to stay on the path of more mature and enlightened behaviour.

We tend to be attracted to individuals who are our opposites in the type of protective behaviour they employ; so you find aggres-sion with passivity, introversion with extroversion, exhibitionism with inhibition, perfectionism with carelessness, pleasing others with only pleasing self. There is wisdom in this selection process because the opposing kind of protective behaviour serves to reinforce our own protective pattern. For example, the person who is passive is strengthened in her protective strategy by being attached to a partner who is aggressive, and vice versa.

Where friends, partners, couples or colleagues display opposite protective behaviours, interpersonal conflict may not arise until some emotional change occurs in one of the parties. But while interpersonal conflict may not be manifested, personal conflict is always present and is continually being manifested in the protective nature of the behaviours operating between the individuals in the relationship. In relationships where the partners are frequently fighting and arguing, the interpersonal conflict is often caused by both of them employing the same protective tactics of aggres-siveness, domination and control. The hidden vulnerabilities of both persons in such a relationship are constantly under threat, leading to escalation of their aggressiveness towards each other in an effort to maintain the protection. While unhappy, and in spite of the continual fighting, such a couple are likely to remain tied to each other because neither has the emotional wherewithal to confront either the other person or themselves. The signals for change are there in the conflict for both of them to see, but as long as they project blame on to each other such insight is blocked. The projection of blame reveals that neither partner is ready for the revelation of his or her vulnerability and dependence, and that safety is needed before either can open up to that journey of discovery.

Interpersonal conflict is more than what it seems

It is my belief that interpersonal conflict is a manifestation of and a protection against deeper emotional conflicts. It is these latter conflicts that need to be the target for change. When the emotional issues are confronted the interpersonal conflict dissolves. When interpersonal conflict is present – no matter its kind – it means that:

- □ Currently used protective behaviours may be under threat.
- □ There may be an escalation of old protective behaviours, or new ones may emerge.
- □ The interpersonal conflict may serve as a protection whereby the couple may be blaming each other, or one is blaming and the other is taking on the blame.
- □ A creative opportunity is provided for both persons to break out of the cycle of protective behaviours by finding safety, and then facing and resolving inner emotional conflicts and moving on to a more open cycle of interpersonal behaviours.

Typical protective interpersonal actions

When any relationship (for example couple, friendships, parent-child, sibling–sibling, colleague–colleague, employer–employee) is troubled, then both parties may engage in one or several of the following protective relationship patterns:

- □ 'being busy' syndrome
- □ taboo issues
- □ projection
- □ introjection
- □ triangulation
- □ arguments over everyday activities
- □ avoidance
- □ displacement.

'Being busy' syndrome

A frequent protection that people use in relationships is 'being busy'. This severely restricts the time for emotional closeness, which would threaten the self-esteem of both persons. Being tied up with your job, domestic activities, hobbies or charitable work provides the rationalisation for 'not having time' for emotional relating. It is important to note that the other person in the relationship colludes with the partner or friend who is 'always busy'. The other person is also engaging in a protective strategy (perhaps overinvolvement with children, zealous religious activity or absorption in some non-emotional hobby such as reading) and it suits that her partner does not put pressure for intimacy in the relationship. This 'being busy' pattern alerts the two people to their individual insecurities, and their present need for protection against the intimacy they fear will bring rejection. The possibility for change in the relationship will emerge only when one of the parties becomes aware of the emotional conflicts, realises the need for self-change and begins to assert intimacy needs in the relationship. Until this happens, the relationship will remain stuck in the protective cycle and deepening of emotional relating is not possible.

Taboo issues

These areas occur when there are issues that threaten not only the self-esteem of the individuals in the relationship but also the tenuous security of the relationship between them. Phrases such as 'don't mention my mother' or 'don't bring up the topic of sex' or 'don't mention your need to go out with friends of your own' or 'leave the past alone' or 'don't bring up yesterday's argument' reflect the presence of prohibited areas within relationships. There is a male client of mine who dares not raise with his wife the issue of his mother-in-law's invasiveness of their home. Such assertiveness on his part would be greeted with rage and blame and, because of his own poor acceptance of himself, it is safer for him to refrain from confrontation. His wife's unhealthy attachment to her mother reveals her continuing childish dependence on her and her own low appreciation of herself. To confront her mother's interference would mean risking rejection by her and to protect against this feared hurt and also possible similar rejection by her husband, the banned topic 'don't mention my mother' comes into existence. Her husband's passivity colludes with her protective strategy and so the alerting signals of the forbidden area go unnoticed by both persons.

Projection

This is the most common protective strategy employed in troubled relationships. Projection is manifested in the following patterns of relating:

- ☐ Blaming ('You're impossible to live with!')
- ☐ Controlling ('Do it the way I'm telling you!')
- ☐ Giving protective criticism ('You're just bone lazy!')
- ☐ Dominating ('What you should do is . . . ')
- ☐ Denying responsibility ('It's all your fault!')

- Being aggressive (pushing, shoving, shouting)
- Being sarcastic ('One might as well be invisible around here.')

The main protective functions of the above means of relating are:

- to pass responsibility for the relationship to the other person
- to take the spotlight off yourself
- to eliminate the possibility of rejection
- to avoid facing up to your own vulnerability.

Implicitly, these patterns of behaviours have the function of alerting you:

- to your own vulnerabilities
- to the need to take responsibility to grow from your vulnerabilities.

A typical example of a protective relationship, wherein one party employs projection, is the deeply insecure male boss who shouts and roars for efficiency from a female staff member, who is insensitive to the frightened and hurt response of the target of his aggressiveness, and who refuses to take responsibility for any inefficiency on his part. Of course, the staff member who reacts passively to such abusive behaviours is protecting herself from further hurt and humiliation by introjecting the critical, aggressive feedback from her boss. By not facing up to her own insecurities, she avoids taking on the threatening responsibility of resolving her hidden conflicts.

It never ceases to amaze me how opposites attract each other and how the strangest of behaviour in one person finds its counterpart in another. But there is method in such a seemingly mad selection process, because each partner needs to learn something of the other's way of operating in life. For example, the person who is aggressive and who is involved with somebody passive, reserved and quiet needs to learn some of the 'holding back' of the passive partner. Conversely, the person who is passive needs to learn some of the 'letting go' of the aggressive partner. However, such maturity will emerge only when one or other or both face up to their individual internal emotional chaos.

Introjection

In recent years there has been considerable progress made in establishing an anti-bullying policy within homes, schools and communities, and not before time! However, to my mind, an even more important campaign needs to be waged and that is against passivity. So many crimes against self and others are committed unwittingly under such banners as: 'for the sake of peace', 'don't upset your father (or mother)', 'don't rock the boat', 'let sleeping dogs lie', 'turn a blind eye', or 'count yourself lucky'. Passivity is an integral part of introjection, because the person who introjects is consistently turning a blind eye to the need to take responsibility for her own vulnerabilities. The effects of introjection, while less visible than those of projection, can be equally devastating to the mature development of yourself and of children and other adults with whom you are involved.

It is a common phenomenon for the parent who is aggressive, dominating and controlling to be seen as the 'demon' in the family while the parent who is passive and acts the martyr is seen as the 'saint'. Nothing is further from the truth – the parent who employs passivity as a protective strategy is as much a 'demon' (albeit unwittingly) as her aggressive partner. I often have to point out to clients the sad fact that not only did the passive parent fail to protect them from the abusive behaviour of the other parent, but also colluded with the abuse by not confronting the unacceptable, and sometimes hugely damaging, behaviours. Of course, just like the person who projects, the parent who introjects is not deliberately neglectful. This person will be able to engage in the confrontation necessary to bring about marital and family harmony only when she faces up to inner hurts. Introjection then is a protection against further hurt, a protection which takes the form of acceptance of abuse from others as in the examples below:

- Pleasing others at a cost to self
- Being non-assertive about your needs
- Being emotionally withdrawn
- Not confronting abusive behaviours towards children or adults
- Being shy
- Being continually apologetic
- Being very reserved
- Being very quiet
- Threatening to hurt yourself
- Having frequent bouts of crying

Such introjecting behaviours serve the protective functions of:

- protection from failure, hurt and rejection (with no confrontation there can be no pain!)
- protection from facing the responsibilty of healing one's own vulnerabilities ('If I'm so useless and worthless, how could I manage such a difficult task?').

The more important alerting messages of introjection are:

- discover your own hidden conflicts
- realise that these conflicts need not be a source of hurt to others
- own and take responsibility for these conflicts.

Triangulation

Triangulation is an immensely clever strategy for protecting against hurt and rejection. An example of triangulation is where the wife in a troubled marital relationship has an extramarital affair and thereby finds a way out of having to confront her spouse about unmet needs and thus eliminates any possibility of rejection. If, when the affair is discovered, the husband, rather than insisting on a serious consideration of their marital relationship, attacks and blames the third party, he now has also discovered a way within the triangle to protect himself, not only from possible further hurt from his partner, but also from facing up to the problems in the marriage, within himself and indeed within his partner. Everybody loses, even the third party, because he now becomes the 'soft-touch' scapegoat for the erring wife and the 'punch-bag' scapegoat for the neglected husband. Until each partner (or even just one) faces up to the reality of their individual and marital problems, it is unlikely the triangle will be broken or, even if it is, some other protective means will be adopted by both partners.

Triangulation is not peculiar to marital relationships but can occur in all interpersonal relationships. A child can become triangulated in a troubled parental relationship, a colleague can become the confidant for an employee having difficulties with a boss, a mother or potential mother-in-law can become the third point in the triangle for a son or daughter in a troubled relationship. In the last triangle, the mother or potential mother-in-law may have her own hidden agenda of holding on to her son or daughter. This situation can be depicted as follows:

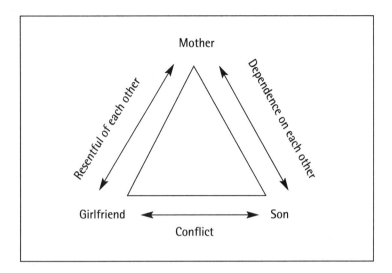

Here the son, rather than facing the difficulties in his relationship with his girlfriend and possible insecurities within himself, turns to the 'safety' of his mother's arms.

Arguments over everyday activities

Some relationships are characterised by frequent rows over such everyday activities as who brings in the coal, cooks the meals, does the washing up, gardens, shops, or cleans the house. The focus on instrumental activities cleverly protects against deeper, more threatening, affective issues becoming the target for discussion. As in the other interpersonal protective actions described so far, there is collusion between the person who complains and the partner who argues with the demands being made, since both are frightened of facing the potentially more explosive emotional issues that lie between and within each of them. As long as it serves its protective function, this pattern of arguing over domestic responsibilities can go on for years. But the pattern of behaviour is also attempting to alert the couple to the hidden issues that need resolution within and between them. The pity is that neither may be ready to face such a prospect and it may take the occurrence of a major crisis to precipitate the changes that are needed to break this protective cycle.

Avoidance

Avoidance is a part of many people's repertoire of behaviours. This is not surprising because avoidance protects against the occurrence of mistakes and failure and the feared consequences of criticism, humiliation, hurt and rejection. The strategy is that when no effort is made or no risk taken, then no failure can ensue. Sometimes the pattern of avoidance is more subtle, where the person aims for the average and stays on the middle path since she feels confident in attaining that level but does not dare to aim higher. The fact that the fear of failure is so common highlights that most people are vulnerable and need to protect themselves from the possibility of further hurt and humiliation. The sadness of it all is that protective avoidance, while it may sometimes be effective in safeguarding against a repeat of childhood hurts, blocks the mature and independent development of people.

Typical avoidance behaviours include:

□ Not taking risks
□ Not expressing needs
□ Bottling up feelings
□ Not being able to say 'no'
□ Turning a blind eye to abuse of others
□ Passively accepting verbal and/or physical abuse from others
□ Rarely initiating social contact with others
□ Waiting for things to happen
□ Dreading change of any kind

- Avoiding the responsibility of facing your own vulnerabilities and interpersonal and other difficulties
- 'Playing it safe'
- Putting on a brave face
- Putting up a pretence
- Always smiling

So many issues are swept under the carpet, passively accepted, brushed over, given a nod and a wink, and quietly forgotten under the banner 'it's none of my business', not with the intent to neglect but to protect. Nevertheless, in many ways avoidance is the biggest tragedy, because it, more than all other protective strategies, perpetuates the non-confrontation of your own personal vulnerabilities. As long as avoidance continues, no personal or interpersonal growth can occur.

Displacement

Many children subconsciously employ displacement as a means of protecting themselves from hurt and rejection mainly by a parent. These children may feel justifiably frustrated and angry at the parent who does not respond lovingly to reasonable needs. The anger is there to help the child voice the need to be loved and listened to, but it is too risky to express this to a parent who has already shown neglect. The anger and frustration may then be displaced on to a sister or brother, or another child or a teacher. It is now well established that children who bully others are themselves very often at the receiving end of similar behaviour by their parents. Furthermore, these children tend to feel insecure, have low self-esteem and fare poorly in academic achievement. The target of bullying behaviour is always somebody who is not emotionally important in the life of the child who is bullying, and therefore there is no great emotional risk in venting her feelings of rage, anger, hurt and humiliation on this person. Teachers and parents need to be alert to such bullying behaviour because it is a clear sign that help is needed, not only for the child who is victimised but also for the child who is bullying.

It is not only anger which may be displaced from its appropriate target. The need to be loved, for example, may be displaced on to non-threatening objects of affection – animals, art, hobbies, interests, job – all of which are things that do not reject you. Likewise, sexual needs may be displaced by adults on to children (paedophilia), animals (bestiality) or objects (fetishes). All such displacement alerts the person to subconscious conflicts that need to be resolved and also provides the necessary protection until enough safety is attained for such inner healing to occur.

HEALING AND PROTECTIVE ACTION

As I have already emphasised, protective interpersonal actions have the function of alerting the person to the need for inner personal healing as well as the need for interpersonal change. However, the protective nature of the behaviours also shows that the person is closed off to such change; she will remain so until an environment that is safe for change is created. Taking on the responsibility for such change is not an easy process but, when adopted, the personal and interpersonal rewards can be very great indeed. The process involved is threefold:

- gaining awareness that interpersonal conflict is an opportunity for healing
- taking the necessary actions to heal your own unresolved inner conflicts
- taking the required steps to heal the way you relate to others.

Personal and interpersonal conflicts are opportunities for change

Overcontrol and undercontrol behaviours and protective means of interpersonal relating are not negative but act like banners, signals or trumpets to draw attention to the need for inner personal healing and, more often than not, to a need to change how you are in your relationships with others. Most people are not aware of this alerting function of so-called negative behaviour and, unfortunately, it is those most in need of change who most stoutly (albeit subconsciously) resist such awareness. Individuals who have some level of self-esteem and reasonably supportive relationships are in a good position to seize the opportunities for change signalled by conflict and seek the means to strengthen their inner selves and their relationships with others. Those who resist the signals for change may seek help only when their protective mechanisms cease to work. Very often such people will need professional help to heal the scars of the past that led them to adopt extreme protective action. The power of the therapeutic relationship can be immense in healing the deep abandonment experienced by these people in childhood. Perhaps for the first time ever, they will experience being loved unconditionally by a fellow human being. The therapeutic relationship provides the fertile ground from which rich healing and growth can occur at both a personal and an interpersonal level. Many of my clients say to me that my understanding of all their actions to date and my recognition of their need for such creative protectiveness help them to stop condemning and rejecting themselves and to start being understanding, compassionate and loving towards themselves.

When conflicting couples come for help and my reaction to their often very sad situation is 'oh happy crisis', they look at me with disbelief because they may have spent the previous weeks or months fighting and arguing or in hostile silence. I recall one such couple who had not spoken to each other for seventeen years. When I began to trace with each of them the origins of their personal vulnerabilities and the necessity for each of them to creatively develop protective actions against further abandonment, they began to see the sense of saying that conflict brings an opportunity for healing and change. They began to understand that each brought the emotional baggage of their individual insecurities and their protective ways of relating to others into the marriage and it was because these emotional issues were unresolved that their relationship became problematic. It is my experience that, when both partners in a conflictual relationship are open to insight and change, separation does not need to occur. Indeed, when both begin to understand each other's journey to date, in a way that they had not seen or appreciated before, their hearts often go out to one another and new beginnings are created in their relationship. Separation needs to be a last option for a troubled relationship, not a first one as is happening so much today.

When a couple do not develop awareness of why their relationship did not succeed, the problem is that they will carry the same emotional baggage into their next relationship and are likely to repeat the same conflict. Sometimes one partner is motivated to explore himself or herself and the troubled relationship but the other person resists such openness. There is no reason why the open partner cannot gain emancipation within himself or herself and within the relationship. Often this partner may now seek a separation so that he or she can continue to grow in maturity and create more fulfilling relationships with others. The partner who is 'stuck' will often not accept this new independence and will increase protective behaviours in an attempt to regain control. I have also worked with couples where both partners were open to insight and change and still chose to separate; they remained supportive and valuing of each other but felt that the differences between them were too great for a fulfilling relationship.

Change always starts with self

When individuals engage in protective means of relating, they are closed off from others. The extent of this will depend on the nature, range, frequency and intensity of the protective inter-personal actions involved. The blocks may be singular or multiple and may seriously hamper one or more areas – emotional, social or sexual – within the relationship. The tracing and undoing of these interpersonal blocks is outlined in later chapters. It will not surprise you to learn that inner personal work needs to precede inter-personal work. When couples come for help, I frequently work with each partner separately to begin with and later on, when each feels ready, we explore their relationship together.

I believe that the basis for all personal and interpersonal protective actions lies within ourselves because each of us has had to develop creative ways to either eliminate or reduce repetitions of our own particular childhood experiences of hurt, abuse, abandonment, guilt and shame. Because each of us has had different childhood experiences, it is necessary to trace our unique histories to be able to heal the hurts of the past. Throughout the book I show how my own childhood experiences shaped me and led me to develop a wide range of protective behaviours that seriously hampered my mature development in adulthood. Other people's stories are given in Chapter 11 in order to help you trace the source of your own protective actions. Getting to the source is vital because success in initiating change lies in finding the causes of our ills and therein finding the necessary cures. But an equally vital ingredient of effective personal change is action. The actions that are needed are unique to each person, but there are common elements to the process of change that we all need to go through. Both the unique and common elements of the process of undoing protective ways and replacing them with openness to self, others and the world are illustrated in later chapters. It may seem an impossible aim but the end point of the journey for each human being needs to be an unconditional love of self and of others, a deep love and appreciation of life, and a realisation of the spiritual nature of the universe and of self. I do believe that an enduring experience of spirituality will begin to emerge only when we have first discovered the wonder of our own being and that of others.

It is my own personal experience, and my experience with many couples over many years, that only when you have learned to celebrate, value, respect, honour, appreciate, nurture, listen to, challenge, praise, affirm and encourage yourself are you then in a position to do likewise for others. Love begins at home with oneself and radiates out from there to others. When there is darkness in your own spirit, then no true light can shine out from you to others.

CHAPTER 7

THE POWER OF STRESS AND ILLNESS

THE BODY IS ALWAYS RIGHT

When a physical symptom reveals an underlying organic disease, people have little difficulty in accepting that the body is right. It is clear that the symptom wisely alerts the person to seek medical help and provides the means for the medical doctor to diagnose the problem. However, people tend to be much more sceptical about the body's rightness in revealing emotional or social problems. Nonetheless, the evidence emerging from psychosomatic medicine, research on stress, psychotherapy, psychoanalysis and alternative medicine is that a high percentage of physical symptoms are emotional or social in origin. What is only rarely appreciated is that signs of stress and psychosomatic illnesses are also protective in nature. The psyche is willing to risk physical well-being in order to protect emotional well-being.

Take, for example, a career woman, married with four adolescent children, who came to me because of frequently occurring blackouts. Her family doctor had sent her to a neurologist, cardiologist and endocrinologist, but no organic basis for her fainting spells could be found. The symptoms continued to worsen and she was terrified that she had some cancer which the medical profession was unable to detect. The increase in the occurrence of the blackouts proved to be a valuable pointer to the psychogenic origin of her symptoms. It emerged that my client rose at 5 a.m. every day, looked after the family and was at work by 8 a.m. Between career and home she worked from early morning to midnight every day, seven days a week, and rarely took a break or holiday. Her blackouts were a perfect metaphor for the 'blacking out of herself' and her driving need to be the perfect mother, wife and successful career person. When she revealed her biographical history, I found a range of other physical symptoms (tension headaches, migraine headaches, blurring of vision, insomnia) had occurred during times when her performance was being scrutinised by others (for example, at school, interviews, examination). Her fear of failure and of disapproval, from parents in childhood and later on from her employer, spouse and children, was exceedingly high and the protective behaviour of perfectionism, of getting it right at any cost, had started at around five years of age. The straw that broke the camel's back, and brought about the serious symptom of frequent blackouts, was that she had been promoted recently and was in dread of 'not being up to it'. She was putting extra pressure on herself to ensure that she measured up. The blackouts acted as an alarm bell to wake her up to the physical extremes she was going to, in order to protect herself. They prompted her to the necessity of finding safety so she could heal her deep dependence problems. Of course, the blackouts also acted as a protection by providing 'a way out', a rationalisation, should she not cope with the job promotion.

When children are emotionally distressed, they are even more likely than adults to speak through their bodies. One of the reasons for this is that they have not yet developed the emotional literacy to express their inner conflicts. Typical symptoms and illnesses that reveal children's insecurities are nail-biting, rocking, bed-wetting, fretting, nausea, stomach pain, nightmares, hyperventilation, asthma, psoriasis. Of course, many adults, and men especially, are also emotionally illiterate and it is their bodies which often reveal their inner fears and insecurities. Male social conditioning where young boys are told not to be 'a sissy', not to be 'a crybaby', to be 'brave and act like a man', has made it unsafe for men to express many of their emergency feelings. The higher incidence of heart disease and suicide among men is linked to this unsafety around the expression of feelings. Feelings provide the energy for the 'fight' or 'flight' response and when this energy is not unleashed it remains, like steam in a blocked kettle, a pressure inside the body and, particularly, within the cardiovascular system.

The body, then, is right not only because it can reveal the emotional and social wounds that need healing, but also because it can act as a protector against recurrences of childhood abandonment and rejection experiences. It needs to be stressed strongly here that the alerting and protective messages of physical symptoms and illnesses are unique and peculiar to the person experiencing them. You cannot say that symptoms such as back pain, tachycardia (abnormal rapidity of heartbeat), high blood pressure, heart disease, arthritis, colitis or irritable bowel syndrome have the same one function for each person. To do this would be to equate the human being to a machine.

Clients sometimes feel ashamed that they have developed psychosomatic illness as a protective force in their lives. But they would not have done so unless it was expedient. The deeper the unsafety and hidden conflicts, the greater the protections need to be. Rather than shame, what I want for my clients is to marvel at the creativity and the complexity of the psyche in its wonderful efforts to alert us to our insecurities and to protect us until we feel safe enough to venture forth and resolve our emotional and social blocks.

Stress as a messenger

The word stress means pressure or strain and it can be physical, psychological or social. Physical stressors include, for example, bodily changes – such as pregnancy, loss of hearing, a broken limb – and aspects of your physical environment such as an overheated room. Psychological stressors arise from within yourself, the most common being dependence on others for approval, repression of abuses suffered in childhood and self-criticism. Social stressors primarily occur in relationships, conflict between people being the most common. Further examples of social stressors include isolation and loneliness. Most stressors are multimodal or biopsychosocial and as such need a holistic response. For example, a woman who, in spite of the pleas of professionals, relatives and friends, returns to an abusive marriage relationship is physically stressed due to the physical violence, socially stressed because of the serious marital conflict and psychologically stressed because of her own poor self-image and dependence on her partner.

When stressors occur, each person will respond in different ways so that the level of stress experienced and the actions taken vary from person to person and from situation to situation. However, there are some common signs that stressors are present. These are the early messengers alerting you to take some protective or healing action in response to the emergency. When you fail to respond constructively to the early signs of stress, the danger is that the signs will worsen and will manifest in the form of physical disease and, if ignored once again, will develop into life-threatening illnesses.

EARLY SIGNS OF STRESS

Behavioural	Accident proneness, drug abuse, temper outbursts, addictive eating or smoking or drinking, loss of appetite, excitability, impulsive behaviour,

$\longrightarrow$

	impaired speech, nervous laughter, restlessness, trembling, rushing about, doing too many things at the one time
Emotional	Anxiety, nervousness, hypersensitivity to criticism, moodiness, apathy, boredom, passivity, depression, frustration, guilt, shame, irritability, loneliness, tension
Cognitive	Obsessive thinking, difficulty in making decisions, lack of concentration, memory difficulties, worrying about task performance, mental blocks, living in the past, future or in a fantasy world
Physical	Accelerated heart rate, high blood pressure, dryness of mouth, sweating, dilation of eye pupils, hot and cold spells, a 'lump in the throat', numbness and tingling sensations, stomach butterflies, tension headache, rapid eye blink

These signs of stress are creative attempts on the part of your psyche to communicate that some change is needed; the particular change involved depends on the nature, frequency, intensity and location of the sign. If the safety is not there to take up the challenge of the change signalled, then the protective function of the stress signs comes to the fore.

One of the most reliable indices of stress is heart rate. Your heart may race with excitement, but unless you are hypochondriacal, you will probably accept it as a normal phenomenon. However, when it races in response to some stressor occurring in your life, then its purpose is to alert you to some personal, interpersonal, occupational or other situation that needs to be resolved. I have worked with a number of clients who regularly checked their heart rate and who panicked at any observed increase. This compulsive checking was triggered by some instance where their heart rate did race and they were frightened by the phenomenon. Rather than seeing the sign as a messenger of the need for some change, they responded with fear of a heart attack or heart disease. With some clients, no matter how much medical and psychological reassurance they got, the preoccupation and checking behaviours continued. I believe that while the initial symptom was a warning about overwork, for example, its continuance was a metaphor for a deeper emotional problem. Not infrequently these clients put their whole hearts into their work but no heart into themselves. The preoccupation with the heart symptom became a symbol for the emotional neglect of themselves and pointed to their need to show heart to themselves. When they began to care for themselves, the compulsive behaviours began to wane and eventually disappeared; they had served their very wise function of drawing attention to the healing needed.

Of course, not all symptoms have such deeper meanings. For example, many people when attending for interview experience a range of stress symptoms, particularly trembling and stomach butterflies. These signs are messages for you to take possession of yourself and to be independent of the interview panel and interview outcome. If you respond with affirmation of yourself and a determination not to confuse your identity either with other people's judgment of you or with interview performance, then the symptoms will abate.

Relationships can be a powerful source of happiness, but can be also a major cause of unhappiness. Early stress signs here may be irritability, discontent, frequent rows and hostile silences. Each is a messenger that some personal or interpersonal change is needed. Hidden conflicts are eating into the well-being of the relationship and the stress signs are attempting to alert you to the challenge of facing them. Many such signals are flown in vain, because individuals do not possess the safety to take on the challenges involved in bringing about a resolution of the relationship problems. When this is the case, the individuals in the relationship take to engaging in protective actions.

Illness as a messenger

One of the saddest times in working with distressed individuals is when someone presents with a serious cancer. While it is now largely accepted that heart disease is a stress-related condition, it is only slowly being recognised that some cancers are also related to chronic stress, such as hopelessness following the death of a loved one. Thirteen per cent of widows and widowers die within six to twenty-four months of the death of their spouse, mostly of cancer. Their cancer signals a dependent relationship with the deceased partner and a lack of any relationship with self. For such people, the prospect of facing life on their own is too daunting and the feeling of hopelessness appears to communicate itself in some as yet undetected way to the immune system. It is as if the immune system picks up the emotional message of 'let me die, I don't want to go on living'.

I recall one young woman, married with three children, who was sent for help at a very advanced stage of cancer. She had been given only a very short time to live. She was married to a man who had been labelled 'manic-depressive' and who had been in and out of psychiatric hospitals all through their married life. She told me that she had no marriage, no sex life, saw no hope for change and felt terribly overburdened and unsupported in the rearing of her three children. Neither did she have any help or support from either her own or her husband's family. She explained to me that for months before the cancer was diagnosed she had been wishing herself dead. The pity is that the earlier signs of distress had not been detected and acted upon, and it took her now life-threatening illness to bring the much deeper disease to light. Sadly, she died within three months of her diagnosis. This poem is an attempt to capture the hidden emotional problems behind the physical manifestations.

Door

She sat in front of me
a woman of unease
looking to me
to set free
death's darkest disease

With life's cord still untied
a frozen smile belying
the rage inside
life denied
silent breath stealing

In myself and others
I had seen her before
without mother
light smothered
knocking at my door

A love that does not bind
the door to bring one hope
that seeks to find
deeper mind
to heal without rope

Some people, lay and professional alike, argue that neither psychological nor social therapies can have any effect on the biological process of cancer or other diseases. What has to be understood here is that the physical disease of cancer is of much shorter duration than the underlying emotional and social disease that has its roots in childhood. Very often there is not enough time to heal the emotional disease before the physical illness ends the person's life. It takes the creation of exceptional safety and a lot of work on the part of both the client and therapist to heal the emotional wounds that have been festering for years. Emotional cuts go far deeper than physical ones.

STRESS-RELATED DISEASES

- Asthma
- Amenorrhoea (absence of menstruation)
- Coronary heart disease
- Brain stroke
- Migraine headaches
- Diabetes mellitus
- Ulcerative colitis
- Skin rashes
- Irritable bowel syndrome
- Back pain
- Essential hypertension
- Cancer
- Retina detachment
- Candida
- Micturition problems (problems passing urine)
- Sexual problems: impotence, frigidity, vaginismus
- Enuresis (incontinence of urine)
- Arthritis
- Alopecia (hair loss)
- Multiple sclerosis (MS)
- Motor neurone disease

Stress-related diseases, like the signs of stress, are messengers for change. Their source lies in a combination of deep inner distress and sad outer circumstances. What is crucial here is the creation of safety so that you can face and heal the emotional issues that your diseased body is signalling so strongly to you. Your movement towards healing will be greatly helped when you have people around you who are accepting and supportive of you.

LANGUAGE, STRESS AND ILLNESS

Even though there has been a reluctance among the medical profession and the social sciences – and among people in general – to accept the notion of psychosomatic conditions and the need for a holistic approach to physical symptoms, our everyday language has always reflected the tie between emotion and body. The accuracy of everyday language in describing the connection between emotion, stress and illness is yet another ingenious 'feather in the cap' of the psyche in terms of its continual strivings for healing and self-actualisation. When you consider that heart disease, which is one of the leading causes of death, is now widely regarded as a stress disorder, it is fascinating to see how often language has made and continues to make the connection between heart discomfort and emotional distress. Examples are:

- □ 'It would make your blood boil.'
- □ 'His heart wasn't in it.'
- □ 'She died of a broken heart.'
- □ 'She was heart-scalded.'
- □ 'I feel such a weight on my chest.'
- □ 'I'm heart-sick.'
- □ 'My heart was in my mouth.'
- □ 'Heart-throb.'
- □ 'Heart of stone.'

Our stomachs too are great revealers of our emotional and social unease. The stomach is the site where many feelings are physically felt. It is remarkable the number of phrases that pick up on this feeling and stomach connection:

- □ 'He hasn't got the guts.'
- □ 'My stomach felt all churned up.'
- □ 'My stomach turned over.'
- □ 'Starved of love and affection.'
- □ 'Hungry for victory.'
- □ 'Constant need to be fed affection.'
- □ 'Knot in my stomach.'
- □ 'Stomach butterflies.'

The back is a very common physical site for adult problems. This is reflected in the following phrases:

- □ 'Put your back into it.'
- □ 'Back off.'
- □ 'Don't get your back up.'
- □ 'Always backing out of things.'
- □ 'It's back-breaking work.'
- □ 'Turning your back on an issue.'
- □ 'Back down.'
- □ 'Back me up in this.'
- □ 'Backed into a corner.'

Respiratory problems (for example, asthma, hyperventilation, hay fever, sinusitis) are common conditions among both children and adults. There is considerable evidence that asthma in children is linked with dominating and overcontrolling parents who do not allow honest and open expression of a range of emergency feelings. Language again has long spelt out the connection between emotional conflict and respiration.

- □ 'I feel all choked up.'
- □ 'Cough it up.'
- □ 'I'm feeling suffocated by you.'

- 'I can't breathe without her knowing it.'
- 'Choking on his words.'
- 'Swallowing one's feelings.'
- 'Don't breathe a word of this to anyone.'
- 'Driven to fever pitch.'

Further examples of how our language uses bodily expressions to describe emotional conflict are given below for different physical organs.

PHYSICAL ORGAN	PHRASE
Bowel	- 'I feel shitty.' - 'He's in the shits.' - 'Pain in the ass.' - 'Tight-assed.' - 'Doesn't know his ass from his elbow.'
Mouth	- 'Tight-lipped.' - 'Poisonous tongue.' - 'Bite the bullet.' - 'Get your teeth into it.' - 'No taste for living.' - 'Sick to the back teeth.'
Eyes	- 'Turns a blind eye.' - 'Shuts his eyes to reality.' - 'Love is blind and marriage is an eye-opener.' - 'Eyes are the window of the soul.'
Neck	- 'Pain in the neck.' - 'Stiff-necked.' - 'Rubber-neck.'
Ears	- 'Turns a deaf ear to it all.' - 'I'm all ears.' - 'Deaf to my pleas.'

→

Genito-urinary system	☐ 'Your bladder is next to your eyes.'
	☐ 'Piss off.'
	☐ 'You're a right prick.'
Skin	☐ 'Thick-skinned.'
	☐ 'Thin-skinned.'
Blood	☐ 'Hot-blooded.'
	☐ 'Make your blood run cold.'
	☐ 'Cold-blooded.'

There are other phrases that indicate the presence of more serious emotional conflicts. When I hear such phrases from clients, colleagues, family or friends, I am alerted to a very serious cry for safety and healing.

☐ 'I'm all eaten up inside.'
☐ 'I'm an emotional cripple.'
☐ 'I feel dead inside.'
☐ 'I have to tip-toe around my partner.'
☐ 'I'm full of bile.'
☐ 'I feel constantly weighed down.'

THE BODY AS A PROTECTOR

You have seen in earlier chapters how the head protects the heart. The body also protects the heart in that it too attempts to eliminate or reduce threats to self-esteem. As indicated above, this is very evident in children. Children can unconsciously manufacture a range of physical symptoms and illnesses in order to avoid the more serious threats of hurt and rejection. The symptoms or illnesses may gain children the attention and nurturing that they are not getting when illness is not present. As one male client put it, 'my mother was happiest and at her most giving when I was ill'. The symptoms and illnesses may also serve the purpose for the child of reducing the shouting, blaming, criticism, violence or sexual abuse that may be occurring in the home. A further function may be to provide escape from doing assigned tasks or going some place which is threatening to their emotional well-being: for example, going to school, staying with relatives, being left with a child-minder who does not like or is punishing of them. Sometimes children's symptoms and illnesses are an attempt to distract parents from the conflict between them. Such conflict can greatly threaten their security because children cannot envisage surviving without their parents.

Just as for children, so it is for adults that the physical symptoms and illnesses which are so important in signalling threats to emotional and social well-being also have a protective power. Adults who have low self-esteem and unresolved childhood conflicts are more likely to use the protective power rather than the alerting power of bodily symptoms and illness. The frequency, intensity, duration and seriousness of the presenting bodily signals are determined by the level of perceived threat and the consequent protection needed.

Sixty per cent of lost work-time is due to lower back pain. In the 1960s disc operations were very common until it was recognised that most lower back pain is psychogenic. But how does back pain protect? I suffered from recurrent back pain for several years and still get twinges. The ready explanation for my back pain was overwork and that certainly was a reality. However, it was a deeper emotional issue – a protective inability to say 'no' to people who needed help – which was the driving force behind the long hours working. This emotional vulnerability can be traced back to my childhood, where I got my recognition and regard by being the 'carer' in the family. My mother was an invalid and there was a ready-made carer role for someone in the family to fall into and I, unconsciously, was the one to fall for it. The role I adopted afforded me protection against rejection and gained me conditional recognition. Relatives and neighbours used to say: 'What a wonderful child, he washes and dresses his mother, cooks the meals, cleans the house, does the shopping.' I was seven years of age! No wonder as an adult I held on to the role of 'wonderful carer' and was reluctant to let go of it. Clearly, the back pain arose to alert and protect me from these emotional issues. As a carer you are always saying 'yes' to others but, of course, always saying 'no' to self. The alerting message was to 'stop carrying the world on your back' and take time and care for myself – to strike a balance. The protective function of the back pain was that, at least, it gave me respite from the tireless giving – the only 'care' was three to four days' bed rest. It afforded me a justifiable way out of having to be always there for others. The enforced bed rest also provided me (when I found some level of safety) with time to reflect and plan change.

Job absenteeism owing to back pain is an effective protective measure against having to face into the everyday stressors and dissatisfactions of work. It affords rest, respite and build-up of energy. Criticism and judgment of these absentees as 'wasters', 'shirkers', 'malingerers', 'useless', 'worthless', 'a burden', only create greater unsafety and the necessity for an increase in the protective back pain. Only when there is safety – both personal and interpersonal – will the person exhibiting the back pain be able to face and resolve the emotional conflict that the symptom signals.

Stress as a protector

You have seen how stress symptoms are an attempt to alert you to the need for changes in your life. But if you are not ready for the challenges of change, you will then respond to the protective function of the stress sign. For example, nervousness and trembling before an interview become the protectors against the possible eventuality of failure: 'How could I have done well when I was so nervous?' But in your protectiveness you miss the opportunity to resolve the real reason for your nervousness, and so the protective stress signs will arise again when the next interview comes up. A common stress sign is that of rushing and racing about. Stop in the street sometime and watch the intensity and strain on people's faces as they rush by you. The rushing and racing is a protection against the possibility of threats to self-esteem such as failure, criticism and rejection. This pleasing of others, in order to avoid rejection and gain acceptance, will not be reduced until you find the safety to pay heed to the alerting message of the stress sign, and begin to resolve your dependence on others.

Hypersensitivity to criticism is a stress reaction with which most of us can identify. While its alerting function is to help you to separate out from the judgment of others, its protective function is to try to control the other person's potential to hurt you. People do, indeed, respond to the person who is hypersensitive with such statements as: 'you can't say boo to her or she'll cry', or 'you daren't contradict him': the protective symptom of vulnerability is now fulfilling its function.

A tension headache may have the protective function of reducing either your own unrealistic demands on yourself or the demands of others on you. The tension headache may compel you to take some rest, express a need or delegate responsibility.

As noted earlier, accelerated heart rate is a common and reliable indicator of stress and strain. How could such a physical reaction be protective? Consider what you do when you notice this symptom. More often than not, you will stop what you have been doing, which is an immediate protective response. You may go to a medical doctor or supportive colleague or friend to complain about your symptom. The heart-racing now becomes the passport or ticket into the doctor's surgery or your friend's confidence – yet another protective function. You may be advised to take some rest and even some medication – further protective results. A major protective function can be that the symptom distracts you from the much deeper emotional and social issues that need to be faced.

Dryness of the mouth often occurs either prior to or during a situation where you are required to speak before others. Fear of their judgment or the threat of failure are what underlie the appearance of the stress sign. The immediate protective response to dryness of the mouth is to wet your lips or ask for a drink of water; this now makes it easier for you to perform and reduces the possibility of failure (for example, becoming tongue-tied). If the verbal presentation is a major threat to your emotional well-being, then other symptoms will appear with back-up protective potential – for example, hands trembling, heart racing, stomach butterflies. In some cases, the stress symptoms may be so intense that they provide the excuse for the ultimate protection of all, which is total avoidance of the situation.

Excessive perspiration is a clear signal for 'cooling down', a necessary protective action when you are under pressure. You may take a drink of water, move into the shade, loosen your clothing, untie your shirt collar, open a window – all of which reduce the strain for you.

It can be seen then that an important protective function of many stress symptoms is that they provide the impetus for the intense preparation, overeffort and perfectionism that avoid threats of failure. You make greater efforts to stay in control, you breathe more deeply, you steel yourself for the challenge, you lean on nearby furniture for support – all protective responses. A number of women with whom I have worked used a pram, trolley or go-car as a protective support for their excursions from home. Only when I felt that they had begun to learn self-support did I encourage letting go of the protective external support. Appreciate the wisdom of your body in providing an 'out' for you, but do remember that the symptoms will keep recurring in a protective cycle until you resolve the hidden issues behind their occurrence.

Illness as a protector

It is a much more serious situation when the psyche, through the body, has to resort to illness as a protector. You have seen earlier that serious psychosomatic illness is the body's attempt to wake you up to deeper emotional and social ills that need resolution. If the necessary safety is not present for facing these deeper issues, the illness instead will provide protection against the threats to your emotional well-being. The psyche is willing to risk physical well-being in order to protect emotional stability. As already mentioned, the prime need of human beings is no longer life preservation but love, recognition and acceptance. Illnesses then can become major protectors against either the reliving or the remembering of past hurts and rejections. People sometimes say that they would prefer to be told they had a serious physical illness rather than a deep emotional problem; this is sensible in a way because the latter poses a greater threat than the former.

I recall a single woman in her thirties who presented with irritable bowel syndrome. Initially, she was very adamant that her illness was purely organic and did not believe in 'any of that nonsense about illness being psychosomatic'. I accepted her protective attitude, because I saw that she was not ready to face her deeper emotional disease. I also saw that her illness protected her from always having to be there for others and gave her some respite from her compulsive caring role. This caring role developed as a means of reducing her mother's aggressive and critical behaviours towards herself, her father and her younger siblings. It was also a means of attaining approval and recognition. These were issues that she faced only when she began to feel safe to express vulnerability with me.

You have seen that lower back pain is a common illness, but then back pain does provide the protective opportunity for 'backing out' of situations that emotionally and socially threaten you. Workplaces and many couple and family relationships are not safe places to be.

Heart disease provides powerful protectors of rest, hospitalisation, relief from pressures, sympathy, nurturance, attention – all the things you had not been giving yourself, or, probably, had not received in childhood. I have helped many men with cardiovascular dysfunction to see how their disease was a necessary and creative development, not only to awaken them to essential changes that were needed in the personal, interpersonal and occupational areas of their lives, but also to protect them from further emotional and indeed physical wear and tear. Those who responded to the challenges survived their physical disease and went on to a more fulfilling and a more holistic approach to living.

It is important therefore that when you experience a physical illness you ask yourself the following questions:

- Is the illness a stress-related disease?
- If it is stress related, what is it attempting to wake you up to?
- If it is stress related, what is it attempting to protect you from?
- If it is stress related, who will provide holistic help?

The presence of a life-threatening or indeed any physical illness demands a fine sensitivity and empathy to what is happening to the person who is ill. In creating safety for openness to the hidden conflicts, a fine balancing of the alerting and protective functions of the illness needs to be maintained. The protective forces must be respected and valued, and only gradually reduced as safety is developed and hidden insecurities are diminished. A close liaison with medical practitioners is advisable since the physical disease, if not curtailed, may well outrun the healing time needed for the emotional disease.

CHAPTER 8

REALISING YOUR POWER

THE POWER OF THE PSYCHE

I am a great believer in the limitless power of the human psyche. In fact, science tells us that we use only about 2 per cent of our brain cells. To say that any human being is a 'fool' or 'stupid' or 'slow' is both grossly inaccurate and damaging to that person's potential. It is true to say individuals may lack certain knowledge and skills, they may come from disadvantaged social and political backgrounds, and they may have limited access to educational opportunities, but these are simply descriptions of circumstances. They say nothing about the vast human potential for learning to create a safe world that allows for growth and development.

The realisation of the great potential of the human psyche to grow and do good is largely determined by the environments into which the person is born. Of course, people can 'rise above' unfavourable environmental circumstances through fortunate relationships, education, wealth, democratic governments and psychological and social therapies, but none of these 'liberators' has the complete answer. Wealth, for example, may free you from limiting physical, social and educational privations, but may not buy you happiness, contentment and fulfilment. Similarly, therapy can enable you to free yourself from the hurts, expectations and conditionality of childhood relationships, but may not offer deeper philosophical and spiritual fulfilment. Political revolutions which promise

freedom and prosperity may take on many of the restrictive characteristics of the old regime. Nevertheless, each of these sources
of liberation does provide a stepping stone to the realisation of
your power. When sufficient personal, social, educational and political safety is present, then the human psyche is free to explore the
inner world of its own capacities and come to some sense of both
personal and universal meaning.

Human beings always want to actualise their potential but, as you
have seen, much of human energy and creativity is spent in protecting ourselves and others from recurrence of experiences of hurt,
rejection and neglect. The more individuals are pushed into emotional, social and political protectiveness, the less opportunity there
is for using the psyche's power to grow. Indeed, the very areas where
you engage in protective emotional, behavioural and cognitive activities are the areas where little or no growth can occur. Nonetheless,
it is important to give credit to the human psyche for its ingenuity
in protecting itself in the unsafe circumstances which constantly
bombard it. Equally, it is astounding to witness the power of the
psyche to grow in situations where safety abides.

In order to best utilise the power of the human psyche – whether
in being protective or proactive – it is important to realise that
this power has several levels of operation. Too much emphasis is
put on consciousness, particularly in Western culture, and contact
is lost with the deeper subconscious and unconscious driving forces
of the psyche. It is high time for these deeper levels of power to
be redeemed from the stranglehold of the rationalism of modern
philosophy, psychology and sociology.

KNOWING YOUR POWER

In exploring human power, it can be useful to think of it in terms
of intrapsychic and extrapsychic; intrapsychic refers to those

biological and psychological powers that reside within the person, while extrapsychic powers arise from the human being's social functioning, and involve the multiple relationships that are part and parcel of the particular culture into which you are born. Children, in their drive towards self-actualisation, are very vulnerable to the effects of the relationships they experience. But even children engage in their own intrapsychic activity to effect progress in their lives. However, there is a much more powerful interaction and bi-directional flow between extrapsychic influences and intrapsychic power in adults (see Figure 8.1). People with low self-esteem and deep unhealed wounds from childhood learn to offset the impoverishing influence of relationships (of partners, parents, bosses, neighbours, criminals, government officials) by protective behaviours operating at conscious, preconscious and subconscious intrapsychic power levels. Avoidance, aggression, manipulation, domination, control and inflexibility are examples of such protections.

FIGURE 8.1: THE INTERACTION BETWEEN INTRAPSYCHIC AND EXTRAPSYCHIC (SOCIAL SYSTEMS) POWER ZONES

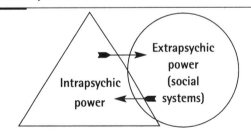

Clearly intrapsychic and extrapsychic powers do not operate independently of each other, but interact in multiple and intricate ways. The tendency to compartmentalise the study of human behaviour into biology, psychology and sociology has not benefited the well-being of people. More and more the push within health, education, social services, industry and so on is towards a holistic orientation, which views the person in total as a biopsychosocial being.

At present we are aware of five levels of intrapsychic functioning. These levels are interrelated in a two-way flow (see Figure 8.2: Pyramid of intrapsychic power, p. 146) and are influenced in turn – again in a two-way flow – by the extrapsychic social and biological environments of which we are a part (see Figure 8.1, p. 137). The five levels of intrapsychic functioning are:

- physical
- conscious
- preconscious
- subconscious
- unconscious.

Physical power

Physical power is connected with energy, health, strength and fitness. It is interesting that we tend to be much more aware of physical power when we are either losing it or are blocked from using it. We take it so much for granted until, for example, a bout of influenza lays us low and then we are very much aware of the gift of energy and how extremely helpless we are without it. Ironically, human beings spend much more time neurotically exhausting their energy than joyfully celebrating, valuing and caring for it.

In Western culture, much money is spent on both orthodox and alternative therapies in an attempt to maintain energy levels. The best-selling drugs are tranquillisers. The vast sales of illicit drugs are maintained not only by those who 'drop out' of responsible living but also by those who put excessive demands on themselves in order to maintain a high workrate, high social performance and high lifestyle. The proliferation of alternative therapies – for example, acupuncture, transcendental meditation, hypnosis, homeopathy, herbalism, reflexology and chiropractice – is in no small way due to the failure of orthodox medicine to deal with the psychosomatic illnesses of our times, and a growing awareness of the side-effects of medication on people's health. Whilst the alternatives are certainly not dangerous to physical well-being, they are providing a similar reinforcement of the neurotic ills of Western society. People are still looking outside themselves for answers to their fears, dependencies and unresolved conflicts, and the protective cycle of living in an unsafe world is maintained.

Certainly a healthy lifestyle, nurturing diet and exercise will do a lot to maintain physical power, but its level can be seriously depleted by protective demands at other intrapsychic levels. For example, people who are deeply depressed may be physically fit but have no energy to do anything. Their physical energy is blocked by a greater need – either at a conscious, preconscious or subconscious level – to protect themselves from the kind of active engagement in life that would threaten their emotional and social well-being. Unless the hidden conflicts being manifested in the depressive symptoms are resolved, it is unlikely that the blocked energy will be released. It can happen, though rarely in my experience, that psychotropic medication will break through the depression, produce some elevation in energy and mood and provide a degree of safety for people to act on their world again. However, such biological intervention does not get to the cause of the depression, and the well-known revolving door of psychiatry is likely to start swinging again. The blocked energy may also be due to the extrapsychic circumstance of an oppressive relationship. But, more often than not, people who suffer domination and control by others are also in need of intrapsychic healing, particularly at the subconscious level of self-esteem.

Physical energy can be enhanced by emotional maturity, independence, a sense of being in charge of your own life, spiritual experiences, non-conformity, intimate relationships and a satisfying career. In this case, there is a healthy cycle of interrelating between all the intrapsychic levels and between intrapsychic and extrapsychic functioning.

Conscious power

This level of power is the one most recognised and utilised in Western culture. It includes:

□ what you do
□ what you say
□ what you think
□ what you feel.

It involves all the internal and external behaviours and feelings that you consciously or knowingly enact. What is often not realised is that conscious functioning can be driven by deeper levels of intrapsychic functioning or can be determined by social forces outside yourself. Nonetheless, conscious power is a tremendous source, which can be used for either growth or protection depending on the safety you experience in the psychological and social worlds in which you live. You have already seen in Chapters 2 and 4 the power of thinking and attitudes in providing protection. In Chapter 6, the power of actions to protect was explored, while Chapter 5 looked at the creative power of feelings to safeguard you when your emotional and social well-being is threatened. However, when your conscious powers are focused on protection, it means that personal and interpersonal development will be blocked in those areas where protective action is needed. When your conscious powers are free to be applied to growing rather than protection, then the development and learning that can occur at all levels of functioning can be astounding.

It is useful to have some idea of how your conscious functioning is influenced by the other intrapsychic levels. Take, for example, avoidance actions, which are very common: avoidance of new challenges, non-confrontation of unfair practices, non-assertion of needs and passivity. These avoidance behaviours may arise from the preconscious attitudes of dependence on success and on others' approval, and from the subconscious fear of abandonment. I have worked with women who consciously avoided creating heterosexual relationships because of much deeper subconscious feelings arising from sexual abuse by their fathers when they were children. They had repressed these horrific experiences from their consciousness (a wise strategy), but their unconscious power guided them into avoidance of relationships with men, where there was a possibility that the abuse might recur and memories of their first abusive heterosexual relationship with their fathers might begin to surface. Some of these women had developed lesbian relationships – a much safer venture for them – but had no conscious idea of why they found themselves more emotionally and sexually attracted to women than to men.

Similarly, you may experience feelings of fear and panic in social situations but not realise that such protective feelings arise from preconscious feelings of insecurity and lack of confidence, and preconscious attitudes that say 'you shouldn't make a fool of yourself', or 'you shouldn't let yourself down in front of others'. In turn, these preconscious feelings and attitudes arise from your own poor self-image at the subconscious level and your need to protect yourself from recurrence of hurts and humiliation.

Preconscious power

This is the level where powerful feelings and attitudes may be operating to either protect you or promote greater levels of physical health and psychological and social development. These feelings and attitudes lie just outside of awareness, but nevertheless can exert a strong influence on what you consciously do, think, say and feel. Feelings of security and confidence at the preconscious level are the driving force behind healthy ambition, social competence, assertiveness, eagerness for challenges, and fairness and justice at the conscious level. On the other hand, deep preconscious feelings of insecurity necessitate at the conscious level protective actions such as avoidance, passivity, aggression, manipulation, compensation or perfectionism.

The preconscious attitudes of 'shoulds', 'should nots', 'have tos', 'don'ts', 'musts' are protective in nature and produce further protective actions at a conscious level. For example, the preconscious attitude 'I should be perfect' leads to conscious behaviours of worrying about performance, feelings of fear when confronted with the need to perform, and verbalisations that either cover up your vulnerability or attempt to justify your avoidance or compensatory actions.

Subconscious power

It is the realm of the subconscious, which contains the awesome power of the need for love and assurance, that is the driving force of many of the activities at the upper levels of the psyche. When this need is met in early childhood by parents and significant others, and later on during school years by teachers and peers, and finally in adulthood by self, the blossoming of the psyche knows no bounds. However, when the subconscious need for love and assurance is either partially or totally neglected, then the world becomes a very unsafe place and the subconscious creates its protection against rejection by developing the fear of abandonment. This protective fear of abandonment, whether arising from partial or total rejection, will permeate all the upper levels of intrapsychic functioning and will be a major factor in determining the influence of extrapsychic forces, particularly relationships. For instance, a woman who was regularly physically assaulted by her father during her childhood and teenage years has not only experienced great loss of love and consequent overwhelming fear of abandonment, but now in adulthood also lives in a very unsafe world where other men could also emotionally and physically abuse her. The first heterosexual relationship a woman experiences is with her father: when this has been of an abusive nature, the psyche wisely surmises that such relationships are a great threat to well-being and will protect her in so many ways, until she feels safe enough to reach out again. In the meantime the following protectors will be maintained:

- Subconscious fear of abandonment
- Preconscious feelings of insecurity, threat and rage when in the company of men
- Preconscious attitudes of 'I'm useless', 'I'm worthless', 'no man would have anything to do with me'
- Conscious feelings of fear in heterosexual situations and feelings of guilt for having hate feelings towards her father
- Conscious thoughts of 'I'm unattractive', 'men don't like me', 'I'd never want to marry'
- Conscious talking about being uncomfortable and unsure of self in the company of men
- Conscious action of avoidance of contact with men, avoidance of confrontation of the unresolved conflicts within her and creation of intimate relationships with women
- Poor physical health and possible cancer risk

The poor physical health protects against further physical abuse – 'you would not hit somebody who's already down, would you?'

The onset of serious illness may bring about the resolution of the problem. As one young woman put it to me: 'Why is it I had to get cancer before my father told me he loved me?' Why indeed! Unfortunately, sometimes even cancer does not bring about the healing the person so ardently desires.

Unconscious power

The power that resides in the unconscious is in my opinion the wisest and most influential of all. The unconscious part of the psyche has an unremitting need to self-actualise and to find meaning. The language of the unconscious is metaphorical – the only universal language that exists. It can encapsulate its needs and frustrations in brilliantly created metaphors. Dreams are but one of the means that the unconscious has of revealing its desires. Typically, when I am under stress myself, I dream of earthquakes. The metaphorical message is clear: 'Will you please deal with the upheavals currently going on in your life, so that further progress along the track of self-actualisation and universal meaning can be attained.' Of course, the power of the unconscious mind is not restricted to dream-time. When its progress is seriously blocked, it can reveal itself through hallucinations and delusions, which, when their metaphorical meaning is explored, can reveal the distressed person's problems.

I recall a young man who was deluded that everybody in Ireland knew about him, that he was the object of a special study and that leading television personalities wanted to interview him. In reality nobody knew of him; he had been found half-starved (another metaphor) and deluded in rented accommodation in a university city. When I met the young man's parents, his mother quite matter of factly said to me: 'I was afraid of giving him a swelled head if I praised him too much.' His father was a distant, silent and unapproachable figure. The young man's delusions now made total sense: in his delusional world he was the central figure, whereas in the real world he was invisible. The delusions represented strong metaphorical messages from his unconscious about his unmet need to be seen and loved, and were an attempt to bring this very serious block to his self-actualisation to the attention of somebody who would understand and provide safety and healing.

The unconscious can guide you into the type of career that represents what you need to do for yourself or that provides the ideal situation within which you can resolve your hidden conflicts. In my own life I seem to have been driven into caring professions – the priesthood, teaching and therapy. I now believe that these professions metaphorically represented my own need to care for myself. I recall one young woman who dreaded any contact with men (her father had been unbelievably cruel to her) and yet at the time she came for help she was a teacher in an all-male school with, apart from herself, an all-male staff. It was the wisdom of her unconscious to provide the perfect setting for resolving her experience of rejection by her father and finding the safety to establish intimacy with men.

The pyramid of intrapsychic powers

As you have seen, human power manifests itself at five levels of intrapsychic functioning that interact with one another, the most potent sources of power being at the subconscious and unconscious levels. These levels are illustrated in Figure 8.2, over. The bi-directional arrows at the boundaries of the levels indicate the two-way interactions between them. Opposite each power level I have listed some of the therapies that focus on that particular level of functioning.

FIGURE 8.2: PYRAMID OF INTRAPSYCHIC POWER

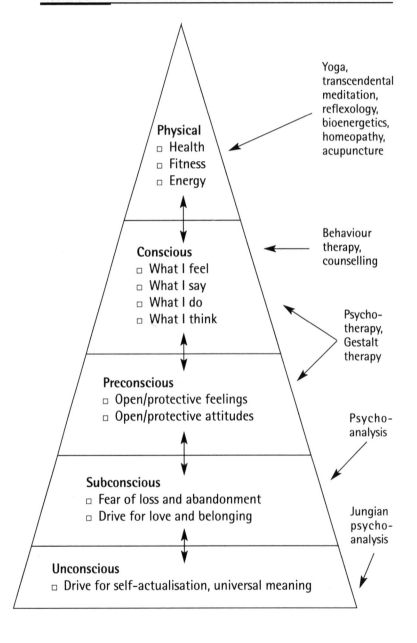

There is often an assumption among both 'orthodox' and 'alternative' practitioners that help directed at one level of power will affect all the other levels. A case illustration may clarify that this assumption is unwise. A young male client of mine, John, presented initially with high blood pressure and a duodenal ulcer (diminished physical power), and intense overworking, anxious thoughts and worry about his work performance and social competence (protective conscious power). On further therapeutic exploration, it emerged that John possessed preconscious rigid attitudes of perfectionism and preconscious feelings of threat and insecurity in work, social and athletic situations (protective preconscious power) and that he had poor self-esteem and an overwhelming fear of abandonment, due to never having 'been good enough' for either of his parents (protective subconscious power). His high blood pressure and stomach ulcer were metaphorically crying out (alerting unconscious power) his need to change from protective high dependence on others' approval and the subconscious hunger for recognition and praise to an acceptance of himself and independence of others. There is no doubt that therapies focused on the physical level such as medication, acupuncture, transcendental meditation or homeopathy would have helped this young man but, in my view, they would not have been powerful or holistic enough to heal the deeper levels of his problems. Similarly, if therapy started at the bottom of the pyramid of psychic power – for example, at the subconscious level using psychoanalysis – it is questionable whether this type of long-term help would have relieved the man's life-threatening psychosomatic illnesses as quickly as was needed.

What John needed was a holistic approach that involved all the levels of intrapsychic power and also included the extrapsychic level. The therapy involved the following:

- Physical power: a focus on this area was essential due to the serious 'illness' symptoms. The aim was to reduce the risk to his physical health. John was taught diaphragmatic breathing, deep muscular and mental relaxation, and posture exercises, and was put on a healthy diet of food and rest.
- Subconscious power: the source of John's problem lay at this level. It was necessary to effect some healing of his abandonment conflict before he would have sufficient safety to let go of the wide range of protective feelings, attitudes and behaviours that had been developed at the upper levels of the pyramid of power. The unconditional acceptance and love which John had from me in the therapeutic relationship provided the foundation of safety he needed to be able to use his powers for growth rather than protection. As John gradually internalised my regard for him, he began to develop an unconditional love and acceptance of himself and, slowly but surely, to become independent of parents, authority figures and others whose approval he had so much strived to get.
- Conscious power: as changes began to occur at the subconscious level, John was encouraged and supported in attempting:
  - to time-manage his day so that not only work needs were attended to but also emotional, social, recreational and sexual
  - to exercise more regularly in order to build up more physical fitness
  - to act, when feeling some depth of emotional safety, on the alerting message of any protective thought that might arise; for example, in response to the protective, anxious thought: 'I dread going into work today', he was to counter with: 'I have all the ability to cope with my day's work'
  - to affirm, when feeling secure in himself, his uniqueness and vast capability and to praise his efforts at work and at self-development
  - to assert his own needs at work.

☐ Preconscious power: John's strongest protectors had developed at this level of power – a horror of mistakes and failure, insecurity in the company of authority figures and deep rigid attitudes that prompted extreme perfectionism at the conscious level. Only slowly was John helped to let go of these protective mechanisms. He learned to replace them with feelings of security, to accept mistakes and failures as opportunities for learning and to practise open attitudes of independence of work and other performance as measures of his worth.

The above outline is of course a highly simplified version of John's therapeutic journey. Human problems are complex, and healing them is also a complex process involving all levels of intrapsychic power in interaction with extrapsychic forces.

USING YOUR POWER TO PROTECT

You have seen that, because of unsafety in the worlds in which we live, your psyche is far more involved in protection than in effecting progress. You have seen, too, that your psyche uses all areas of functioning in its task of protection:

☐ protective stress and illnesses
☐ protective conscious feelings
☐ protective conscious thinking
☐ protective conscious actions
☐ protective preconscious feelings
☐ protective preconscious attitudes
☐ protective subconscious fears of abandonment.

As emphasised many times in this book, only when safety is created will you be ready to let go of some or all of these protective behaviours. In letting go it is important to remember how well these strategies have served you and recourse to them may still be needed again in the future. Indeed, as you will see in Chapter 9, personal development and the care of others and of the environment is a delicate interplay between being protective and being safe.

USING YOUR POWER TO GROW

The process involved in using intrapsychic and extrapsychic powers to effect growth is unique to each person. My experience as a therapist has shown me that each client needs a different therapy. You are a unique individual with a biographical history that may have some common elements with others but which is predominantly particular to you. When you see yourself in this way as unique and special, you have already begun the process of creating the safety necessary to be able to employ your powers to grow.

The guidelines given below for enhancing both intrapsychic and extrapsychic powers to grow may or may not suit you at the moment. Do not go against any emergency feelings that may arise when you attempt to engage in any of the suggested actions. Respect your feelings, protect yourself, detect the threat and when you have found safety, try again.

In enhancing intrapsychic power, you are strengthening yourself not only for growing but also for facing any personal, interpersonal or other crises that may arise. The more activated your intrapsychic powers are, the more likely it is that you will see and respond to crises as opportunities for further growth rather than as occasions for retreating into protective actions. Different strengths are needed for different crises and it is wise to give space, time and resources to the development of each level of power. Self-actualisation is an unending process; the more developed your powers are, the further down this road you will travel and the more eager you will be for further challenges.

Enhancing physical power

Given that our bodies are the vessels of everything we are and can become, it is amazing that neglect of our physical welfare is far more common than care. It is true that cosmetic care is common, but genuine care for our bodies is relatively rare. Physical power involves health, strength, stamina, fitness and a strong immune system. The actions that enhance your physical power are not highly demanding but do require regularity and consistency.

- Taking regular physical exercise (30–40 minutes of moderate exercise 4–5 times weekly)
- Resting when tired
- Not exercising beyond tiredness
- Having a nurturing daily diet (avoiding junk foods)
- Dieting to follow your energy pattern (eating when hungry)
- Taking time to digest food after a meal
- Doing things easily and calmly (no rushing and racing)
- Practising diaphragmatic breathing
- Learning a deep relaxation exercise and practising it daily
- When tired, stressed or overburdened, asking for help and support
- Providing a comfortable living space for yourself
- Having a routine sleep pattern of 7–8 hours daily
- Being sensitive to your body's protective messages and responding appropriately
- Time-managing your day in a way that promotes a balanced lifestyle
- Showing concern for the physical welfare of others
- Giving yourself a treat now and again

Enhancing the power of action

Your actions can have profound blocking or enhancing effects on yourself, others and the world. While you are not to blame for your protective actions, you are always responsible for them. The more you consciously engage in actions that promote love, respect, trust, value, acceptance, encouragement, praise, affirmation, assertiveness, responsibility, kindness, caring and discipline, the more safe and challenging your own life and the lives of those with whom you come in contact will become. You will fail at times, lose control, be inconsiderate, neglectful of self or others, aggressive, passive, irritable, dismissive or moody, but these protective actions can be redressed with sincere apologies and a return to caring responses. Remember, too, that what you put into the world of people and things is what you are likely to get back.

Enhancing the power of feeling

If it is actions that most influence the world, it is your conscious feelings that are the surest barometer of how life is for you and are the principal determinant of your internal and external actions. You will recall that your conscious feelings are determined in turn by deeper preconscious and subconscious emotions. How you feel about yourself, others and the world will colour everything you do.

What is paramount then is the development of a deeply caring relationship with yourself at the physical, conscious, preconscious, subconscious and unconscious levels. All human problems come from a lack of love: of self, of others and of the universe. The deeper your loving relationship with yourself, the more caring you can be of others. Love of self, others and the world is the cornerstone of a fulfilling, healthy and long life. It is the force that brings about strong bi-directional flows between all the levels of intrapsychic power (see Figure 8.2) and between intrapsychic and extrapsychic power (see Figure 8.1). It is the *sine qua non* for self-actualisation, enriching relationships, a peaceful world and a fair sharing of the world's resources. Your relationship with self and others needs to mirror that of an unconditional loving relationship between a parent and a child. Much of our adult lives is taken up with correcting the parenting and other relationship experiences we were exposed to as children, so that fears of abandonment, feelings of insecurity and protective attitudes of perfectionism or apathy are transformed and give way to feelings, thoughts, verbal expressions and actions of love, care and challenge.

Enhancing the power of thought

Feelings and actions always speak louder than words or thoughts, and what you feel and do have a greater influence on how you are in this world. Nevertheless, there is much that can be done to enhance the power of thought and imagery and the power of what you say. Thinking and imagining provide you with immense capacities for growing: you can perceive, learn, create, analyse, understand, plan, project, memorise, focus, interpret, reflect, compare and invent. These capacities can be enhanced by:

- Having a love of learning
- Perceiving learning and education as a life-long process
- Seeing mistakes and failures as opportunities for learning
- Reading
- Discussing ideas
- Listening to the ideas and opinions of others
- Experimenting with ideas
- Observing the world
- Living in the present moment
- Developing concentration skills
- Planning time for reading, discussion, education
- Setting intellectual challenges for yourself
- Visiting museums, art galleries, libraries
- Making time for reflection

Enhancing the power of the unconscious

If you become familiar with the metaphorical language of your unconscious, you can respond more readily to its alerting messages regarding blocks to your growth. A useful exercise is to keep a diary of your dreams. Read over them with a metaphorical eye and after a time you will see themes. Reading poetry, myths, legends, fairy tales – all rich in metaphor – can give you a better appreciation of the ingenuity of metaphorical communication.

Enhancing extrapsychic power

With regard to the enhancement of extrapsychic powers, it helps if you surround yourself with people who are life-giving, mature, caring, wise and balanced in outlook, non-conformist, challenging, adventurous, assertive and spiritual. It helps, too, to stay in touch with nature and its bounty so that your appreciation and care of your physical environment grows and matures. As much as your material resources allow, try to live in a physical environment that is life-giving. It is important at all times to seek out places and people that promote safety for your growth and development.

CHAPTER 9

THE POWER OF SAFETY

SAFETY IS THE KEY TO HEALING

The first chapter of this book noted that the world is often not a safe place to be, and that unless safety is present a person cannot move fully towards self-actualisation. In the absence of safety, it is of course only those parts of the adult or child which are traumatised or threatened that will not mature. The rest of the psyche may develop and mature, but a callous of protective emotions, cognition, actions, stress symptoms and perhaps illness closes around the wounded part, leaving it unhealed. The focus of this chapter is to explore how safety can be created so that the traumatised and blocked parts of the psyche can be healed and resume their journey towards maturity.

To judge people as 'lazy', 'irresponsible', 'bad', 'stupid', 'weak', 'aggressive', 'passive', 'mad', 'insane', serves only to further traumatise them and leads to a necessary exacerbation of their protective behaviours at all levels of power. Understanding and compassion are vital in our responses to the protective behaviours of ourselves and others in this world. It is the responsibility of all of us to create safety not only for our own personal development but also for the development of others. The sources of unsafety lie in the reactions of significant adults – particularly in childhood but also in your adult life – to certain behaviours such as making mistakes and failing, showing sexual curiosity, being non-conformist, having temper tantrums, expressing feelings, asserting needs, displaying initiative, daring to be different, not living up to the expectations of significant others.

The weapon most used when we display behaviour displeasing to others is withdrawal of love and, when this happens, the psyche wisely feels threatened and resorts to creative ways of reducing or eliminating the threat. The psyche may now protectively resort to, for example, perfectionism, sexual repression, conformity, passivity, bottling up of feelings, non-assertion of needs, apathy, sameness and desperate efforts to meet the expectations of others. All of these protective responses reduce the threat to the psyche's need to be loved, recognised and valued, but the cost is that you cannot now grow in these blocked areas. However, the protective response is the lesser of two evils since the greatest evil to befall a human being is not to be loved.

For children, safety is created primarily by the significant adults in their lives: parents, teachers, relatives, other family mentors and – later on in their lives – peers. For adults, two levels of safety need to be established: personal and interpersonal. Adults have the advantage over children that they can create a relationship with self and thereby generate personal safety independent of others. However, the healing process is speeded up when interpersonal safety is also established. Interpersonal safety is brought about by compassionate and unconditional relating between people. There are some individuals who have been so grossly neglected and rejected that the safety of the intense, unconditional relationship of therapy is needed before they can progress to the development of their own personal safety and trust the interpersonal safety offered by others.

PERSONAL SAFETY

The creation of personal safety is really only possible for the person whose trauma and protective callous are of a moderate nature. Such people will have matured quite well in the unthreatened areas of their lives and the safety in those areas can be used to heal the threatened layers of being. Gross neglect, when it occurs, tends to be of a very generalised nature so that most aspects of the person's functioning are blocked and very serious levels of immaturity and irresponsibility necessarily result.

The creation of personal safety involves the following process:

- being understanding of and compassionate towards the repertoire of protective physical, conscious, preconscious and subconscious behaviours you have creatively developed over your life
- detecting the traumatised areas of being that need healing
- knowing how and why these wounds were caused
- creating a relationship with yourself that is loving and caring, a relationship like that of an ideal parent to a child.

Being understanding and compassionate

Along with love, compassion is the most healing and life-enhancing emotion. It is different from sympathy because there is a far greater depth of feeling and understanding present. When you experience compassion from another, it is as if this other person knows truly the depth of hurt and pain you have experienced, understands deeply the seemingly hurtful and neglectful behaviours you display at times, and sees right through to the goodness, uniqueness, worth and value of your person. There is no judgment or criticism of you or your behaviour, but there is caring and support for you to lean on while you take on the necessary risks involved in the healing of your traumatised and blocked areas of growth. We need to create that kind of understanding and compassion towards ourselves, our vulnerabilities and our protective strategies.

One of the best ways of doing this is to take yourself by the hand and begin to travel back over the paths that brought you to your present vulnerable place. As you journey, you will eventually come to the starting places of your hurts, traumas and vulnerabilities and you will find a very small hand clutched in your adult hand. You may find – as I do when I write these lines – that you weep and feel such love and compassion for this small child, your heart going out to him. Take this child in your arms; give comfort; listen to the hurts; be there for the child in ways that your parents or others were not there for you. You have now found compassion.

Detecting the traumatised areas that need healing

Each person's story is unique and there is nobody who has not got a story to tell and traumatised areas that need to be detected.

In my own story the traumatised areas were:

- feeling unattractive and ugly
- feeling wanted only when I was pleasing others
- feeling that no one was truly there for me
- feeling that mistakes and failures were a major source of threat
- feeling overburdened with adult responsibilities
- feeling that I was expected to take care of myself.

It is a good idea to write out your story so that you can more easily detect your own particular hurts and vulnerabilities. Once you know these, the healing actions that are needed are easier to define. Reading the stories in Chapter 11 may aid this process for you. If you have a brother or sister who is open to such journeying, then relating your stories to each other can be of enormous help, but you must be sure that both of you can provide safety in the form of love, compassion and non-judgmental responses. It is interesting that, when two members of a family relate their stories, they can often seem as if they came from different families. But this simply bears out the fact that each person responds in unique ways to the dynamics of family relationships. The neglect is real, but how each child responds to it will be different.

Knowing why and how these wounds were caused

For many years I felt bitter towards my parents, not only for my experiences in childhood, but also for again not being there for me when after seven years I left the Catholic monastery I had entered at eighteen years of age. I also felt very angry towards the priests who after seven years left me high and dry, without any finance or guidance on what to do with my life. I did not realise then that my parents and these priests had done their best within the limits of their own traumatised histories. It was only when I began to trace my father's story and my mother's story and the stories of other significant adults in my life that I truly began to realise that they were in no position themselves to offer me the kind of loving and nurturing a child needs. My heart went out to them as I discovered their histories, and my feelings of bitterness and anger were transformed into love and compassion.

I now truly believe that no human being deliberately betrays, neglects, abuses or hurts another human being. I believe that such behaviours come from very abused and traumatised places within people and that they are protective projections out from those dark places. I no longer judge or condemn, but I do not collude and I do confront, but in a way that is caring of myself and of the person exhibiting the abusive behaviour. The 'why' of neglect lies in the traumatised areas that have remained blocked within parents and the other significant adults who perpetrated the neglect. As you have seen, bitterness towards those who neglected you and blaming of the past for the way you now feel about yourself, others and life are major protective preconscious feelings and attitudes. Discovery of the hidden pain in the stories of those who hurt you can soften and even transform these preconscious protectors. Even if you are not in a position to trace these people's histories, you can rest assured that what they did and said was not intentional, but somehow a repeat of the cycle of neglect they had experienced themselves as children. Their behaviours are certainly responsible for your vulnerabilities today, but they are not to blame. Unfortunately, they did not have the safety to be loving and responsible, but you now have the opportunity to take on those most precious responsibilities of loving yourself and others and appreciating the world you live in.

The 'how' of neglect is found in the patterns of behaviour that operated in the family, in the school and in other key relationships. Very often you will find that either you are repeating the neglectful patterns or you have developed psycho-diametrically opposed patterns of behaviour to those who most influenced you; in both cases extremes are present and the neglectful cycle repeats itself. Seeing the repeated neglectful cycle will highlight possible protective responses you may have developed. You will recall that these protective responses are the window through which you can see the hidden vulnerabilities that need to become visible before change can begin. Even more so, seeing the repeated cycle of hurt and pain in your present relationships with yourself and others will give you a clearer and more compassionate perspective on the early origins and architects of your problems.

Creating a relationship with self

Trauma is caused by relationships, particularly those that operate within the family and the school in your early years. Then you were most sensitive to abandonment, criticism, ridicule, scoldings, 'put-down' messages, comparisons with others, silent hostility, threats, aggression, overprotection and betrayal through passivity on the part of those whose responsibility it was to protect you from abuse. When there is no one there to protect, you quickly learn to invent your own protectors. If the causes of your being blocked in particular areas of human functioning are neglectful childhood relationships, it stands to reason that the 'cure' also involves relation-ships – relationships of a nature that promote growth and maturity. It may help enormously if you can find relationships with others that are of a life-giving and unconditional nature. I say 'may', because there are many people who are deeply depressed and distressed in life, even though they are loved by others, because they are not in a safe enough place to risk internalising those love messages.

There is another issue here and that is that as an adult you cannot afford to depend on others to feel good about yourself. To do so would be to repeat childhood dependence (which is why children are so susceptible to even the slightest emotional cut) and would mean that, if those people who show you loving regard should die, or move away, or reduce contact with you, you might find yourself thrown back into trauma again. It is certainly a bonus to have others around you who love you, but the most essential and enduring, mature and strengthening relationship of all is that with yourself. Many people baulk at this suggestion, but this is a protective response to a type of relationship that has not been modelled, encouraged, supported or celebrated in our culture. Nonetheless, it is the key relationship, the one and only relationship that cannot be taken from you. It gives you an appreciation of your own unique self and in turn an appreciation of others, and it gives you an inde-pendence of needing the approval and acceptance of others. The relationship with self is essentially about being there for yourself and not repeating any of the abandonment experiences of your childhood relationships.

Because the relationship with self has not been strongly modelled in our society, many people do not know how to have such a relationship. They say 'how do you mean "love yourself"?' or 'how could you have a relationship with yourself? It sounds ridiculous!' or 'it sounds very selfish'. In regard to the last response, ironically it is when you do not love and appreciate yourself that 'selfishness' (protection) emerges in the forms of possessiveness, control, aggressiveness, passivity, attention-seeking, conditional giving, manipulation, withdrawal, violence, sulks, silent hostility and so on. All these 'selfish' behaviours are designed to enforce recognition from others, but the consequences are extremely damaging of the targeted persons. When you have a fine sense of yourself, what emerges is 'unselfishness', which is manifested in such behaviours as unconditional giving, justice, sincerity, compassion, understanding, assertiveness, genuineness, honesty and concern. Unfortunately 'selfishness' is far more common than 'unselfishness', a fact which underlines the importance of developing a more loving relationship towards ourselves.

The best way to discover how you might develop a loving relationship with yourself is to ask yourself: 'What kind of a relationship would I have wanted my parents to have with me when I was a child?' Recall the small hand you found in your adult hand when you were retracing your life story; it is that neglected child within you who needs to grow and it is only through the safety of your love that the child's traumatised areas have a chance of being healed.

Possible answers to the question above include:

□ Being accepting of my uniqueness
□ Being kind and caring

- ☐ Being unconditionally loving
- ☐ Being gentle
- ☐ Being physically demonstrative of their love for me
- ☐ Being attentive to my needs
- ☐ Listening attentively to me
- ☐ Having fun with me
- ☐ Nurturing me
- ☐ Being positively firm with me
- ☐ Encouraging me
- ☐ Being appreciative of my differences from them and others
- ☐ Believing in my vast potential
- ☐ Being appreciative of my efforts to learn
- ☐ Being fair and just towards me
- ☐ Being understanding of me
- ☐ Praising my efforts rather than my performance
- ☐ Celebrating my specialness
- ☐ Being there to give advice when needed
- ☐ Fostering responsibility in me
- ☐ Being apologetic when they were wrong
- ☐ Being compassionate towards me
- ☐ Acting as good friends
- ☐ Being open and honest about themselves
- ☐ Being real and genuine
- ☐ Being providers of positive experience
- ☐ Being accepting of mistakes and failures as opportunities for learning
- ☐ Being trusting of me
- ☐ Giving me the freedom necessary for me to learn to stand on my own two feet
- ☐ Being accepting of my need for privacy
- ☐ Being appreciative of my need to make my own decisions on issues

- ☐ Being sensitive to my lack of experience and knowledge
- ☐ Being protective in areas where lack of experience and knowledge could get me into trouble
- ☐ Being challenging
- ☐ Being respectful

Quite a tall order but, nonetheless, the list outlines the major features involved in the kind of parent–child relationship that ensures unblocked movement towards self-actualisation for both child and parent. This is also the relationship that you as an adult need to have with yourself. Like a parent–child relationship, it demands persistence and consistency in these caring responses towards yourself on an everyday basis. Go through this list regularly so that you begin to cease the abandonment of yourself and replace it with an enduring unconditional relationship with yourself. It is this relationship with self that is paramount in creating the personal safety you need to be able to face into the traumatised areas within yourself and gradually begin to take the actions necessary to heal the wounds that are there.

INTERPERSONAL SAFETY

While an adult can create personal safety, for a child it is interpersonal safety which is essential. Because of this it is incumbent on parents, and others in charge of children, to ensure that the relationships to which children are exposed in the home, school, community and elsewhere are of an unconditional caring nature. For an adult, interpersonal safety can provide tremendous support, energy, encouragement, affection, warmth, trust and belief in your potential, material resources and affirmation. But it is only the person with personal safety who can create and respond to interpersonal safety. How you relate to yourself determines how you relate to others, and people low in personal safety and self-esteem will tend to fraternise with people like themselves. The converse, of course, is also true.

If you develop a relationship with yourself along the lines given above, you will find that, automatically, you begin to feel uneasy with long-term relationships that are unsafe and have a desire for a different kind of relationship that is more mature in nature. You can take direct action to establish relationships with others that are of a life-giving and safe nature. There are two aspects to approaching this challenge: one is knowing which relationships to avoid and the second is knowing which to foster.

Relationships to avoid are those characterised by the following:

- Possessiveness
- Control
- Domination
- Manipulation
- Aggression
- Passivity
- Judgment
- Conditionality
- Lack of love
- Violence
- Hostility
- Criticism
- Blame
- Neglect
- Lack of challenge
- Disrespect

You might well ask: 'how do I avoid such relationships when I am surrounded by them?' Two issues arise here: you must 'take the stye out of your own eye first' and you must recognise that the behaviours you are avoiding are damaging not only of your development but also of those who exhibit them. You are not rejecting the person of those who protectively relate in the ways listed but, at the same time, you are neither going to seek them out nor collude with them. When you cannot avoid them, it becomes necessary for you to confront and assert your rights to be accepted, recognised and valued. You confront in a way that is caring of the other person, but you definitely do not collude with their protective ways of relating to you. Again, assertiveness and confrontation that is caring but firm is possible only when you have some level of acceptance and recognition of yourself.

While it is important to avoid relationships that do not provide safety for you, it is even more important that you actively seek out people who provide safety.

Relationships that provide safety are characterised by such responses as:

- Respect
- Valuing
- Active listening
- Acceptance
- Kindness
- Patience
- Tolerance
- Unconditional love
- Fairness
- Justice
- Belief in yourself
- Trust
- Responsibility for self
- Maturity

- ☐ Assertiveness
- ☐ Encouragement of effort
- ☐ Praise of effort
- ☐ Affirmation
- ☐ Honesty
- ☐ Openness
- ☐ Genuineness
- ☐ Sincerity
- ☐ Compassion
- ☐ Understanding
- ☐ Positive firmness

The relationship that provides safety is life-giving, non-judgmental and unconditional. You might now ask, 'where am I going to find such a relationship?' Certainly, those relationships to avoid are far more common than those to foster. But this is not a black and white issue and it is important to see that relationships that do and do not provide safety are on a continuum. At least you can pursue the relationships that are at the safe rather than the unsafe end of the continuum. Furthermore, when you behave towards others in the ways listed above, you make it safe for others to be also open and unconditional with you. You need to be patient, however, since it takes time for people (including yourself) with hidden wounds to trust the healing balm of a caring relationship.

THERAPEUTIC SAFETY

There are some individuals who have become so protectively estranged from themselves that it is too threatening for them to risk any attempt at the creation of personal and interpersonal safety. Their earlier childhood experiences have led them to build up protective walls to such an extent that a medieval castle would not match them for defensive strength. It is safer to stay behind the protective walls of isolation, violence, drug abuse, alcohol abuse, overwork, perfectionism, time-consuming hobbies and interests, relentless career ambitions, hallucinations, delusions, religious or political fanaticism, 'selfless' helping of others, psychosomatic illnesses and so on. Such a person, with an inner child suffering untold pain of rejection, needs a special kind of relationship to emerge from behind the protective walls. This is the therapeutic relationship where clients, in spite of the grossness of their protective behaviours, are exposed to an intense, continuous relationship that is unconditionally loving, accepting, valuing and deeply compassionate. This relationship cannot afford to repeat any of the protective characteristics of the clients' childhood relationships because, if it does, the clients will quickly go back into their protective shells. Once the trust is broken, it is very difficult to re-establish. The responsibility on the therapist is enormous and one that must not be taken on lightly. This is the one lifeline that may help these very hurt people to climb outside their protective walls and begin to have some sense of their goodness and worth.

If you are referred to a therapist by your family doctor or a colleague or friend, be sure that you feel safe with the therapist before you begin to expose your protected wounds. When you do not feel safe, voice it so that the therapist will work harder at creating safety for you. If you still feel unsafe, do not be afraid to ask to see another therapist. There are many reasons why safety may not develop between a client and a therapist and these are not all connected with the client. It may be, for example, that the therapist is using a model of psychotherapy that is not suitable for the client. Therapists too are not without their insecurities and, either consciously or subconsciously, a client's particular problem may threaten their protective walls and lead to a distancing from the client. This is not deliberate behaviour, but therapists need to be sensitive to such responses and be open and honest about their reactions to the client. Sometimes this very act of openness can re-establish lines of safety. If you find yourself going from therapist to therapist, a protective response of 'setting up the therapist to fail' may be operating (clever projection – 'it's all the therapist's fault'). It would be wise for you to stick to the therapist with whom you feel safest so that possibilities for change may be allowed to emerge.

The creation of therapeutic safety may take some considerable time, but time is not the issue. Rather it is the patience to maintain the unconditional and compassionate relationship so that eventually the client will see that no matter what he does, thinks, says or feels, the loving hand is still held out to him. If you have had twenty, thirty, forty or more years of hiding behind protective walls, it takes a tremendous level of therapeutic safety to help you to emerge from behind them. I recall many clients who showed no response or were even hostile in the therapeutic relationship for more than a year before a breakthrough occurred. Once the breakthrough has occurred, some level of safety is now there for the actions that are necessary to transform the wounded parts of the client's psyche.

CHAPTER 10

HEALING AND MOVING ON

HEALING AND RELATIONSHIPS

The creation of personal and interpersonal safety and, when necessary, therapeutic safety provides the foundation for the psyche to resume its journey towards maturity in those traumatised areas of living that, up to this point, have had to be protected. Once the safety is there, healing actions can be initiated to address the blocked areas of development. I want to reiterate here that a person is not a machine, nor a victim of heredity, biology, social conditioning or subconscious conflicts, but a powerful being who, when released from having to protect self in an unsafe world, can use these same powers to accelerate the movement towards self-actualisation. It is not lack of power that prevents change but lack of safety.

The healing actions that adults need to engage in are primarily of a personal nature, especially to begin with, and secondarily of an interpersonal nature. The healing actions needed for children who have been traumatised are primarily of an interpersonal nature. Once the significant adults in children's lives persistently and consistently show caring responses towards them, then healing and growth will gradually begin to occur. Adults need to take responsibility for their own healing, whilst not being afraid to seek the support and encouragement of others in this process.

The healing actions that are required will differ from person to person. Each person needs to discover her own traumatised areas and consequent protectors. Possible actions of personal healing are considered in the next section and those of interpersonal healing in the subsequent section. Therapeutic healing is discussed in the final section of this chapter.

PERSONAL HEALING

The essential basis for the personal healing of an adult is the creation of personal safety through an unconditional loving and compassionate relationship with self. Not only does such a relationship provide security, but it means that all your healing actions, thoughts, imaging and self-talk will now be infused with feelings of love, hope, excitement, security, confidence, tenderness, joy and compassion. Without such an infusion of emotion from your preconscious and subconscious feelings, your conscious actions, thoughts, imaging and words will be hollow sounding and have little or no healing impact. Furthermore, if your healing behaviours are not suffused with feeling, not only will they not cure your emotional disease, but neither will they effect a change in any stress or illness symptoms you may have.

A further factor that will enhance your healing process is regular practice of the actions outlined in Chapter 8 which enhance the different levels of physical, conscious, preconscious, subconscious and unconscious power. With these foundations in place, you are now ready to set in motion the specific actions that are needed for your particular wounded parts.

To give you some sense of what is involved here, I have outlined below my own areas of traumatisation, the protectors I developed and the healing actions that have brought me further down the road towards self-actualisation.

WOUNDED PARTS	PROTECTORS	HEALING ACTS
Feeling unattractive and ugly	Avoidance of heterosexual contact, aggression, closed thought patterns, fear and depression	Redeeming of my physical self by acceptance of my uniqueness, heterosexual contact, open thinking, independence of others' opinions, care and nurturing of my body
Feeling wanted only when I was pleasing others	Constant pleasing of others, no expression of my own needs, conditional giving, passivity	Valuing, expressing and meeting my own needs, being assertive, unconditional giving
Feeling that no one was truly there for me	Fear of abandonment, deep insecurity, sadness, isolation, hopelessness	Unconditional love of self, being there for self
Feeling that my needs did not really count	Anger, dissatisfaction, resentment, irritability	Taking responsibility for my own needs, openly revealing my needs to others
Feeling that mistakes and failures were a major source of threat	Perfectionism, overwork, avoidance, anxiety, living in past or future	Separating my person from my behaviour, seeing mistakes and failures as opportunities for learning, living in the present, viewing tasks as challenges

⟶

Feeling of being overburdened with adult responsibilities	'Martyr' behaviours, complaining, never saying 'no', passivity	Separating out from dependence on others, allowing others to take responsibility for themselves, saying 'no' when required, being assertive
Feeling that I was expected to take care of myself	No display of vulnerability, no requests for help or support	Owning and when necessary expressing vulnerability, requesting help and support when required

The most difficult aspects of my journey (and I still struggle with these issues at times) were acceptance of my physical self, feeling confident in heterosexual situations, being there for myself, recognition of my own needs, saying 'no' to demands from others and asking for help and support.

The healing process is a complex and multifaceted task, but one for which you have all the resources you need. Remember if you have been so ably protecting yourself from hurt, humiliation and rejection for all these years, now – when you have found safety – you can use those same ingenious qualities to heal your hidden conflicts.

The *step-by-step journey of healing* can be outlined as follows:

STEPS TO HEALING YOUR WOUNDED SELF

1. Creation of personal safety (provides the essential basis for healing)
2. Creation of interpersonal safety (provides support systems for healing)

3. Enhancement of all your levels of power (provides the power resources for change)

4. Identification of your physical, conscious, preconscious and subconscious protectors (provides a window into your wounded parts and points to the actions needed for healing)

5. Identification of your wounded parts

6. Determination of actions needed to heal wounded parts and let go of protectors

7. Unconditional engagement in healing actions

Throughout this book you have seen how, when you live in unsafe worlds, you creatively and necessarily invent multiple ways of protecting yourself from further wounding. These protectors may operate at the physical (stress and illness), conscious (feelings, thoughts, words and actions), preconscious (feelings and attitudes), subconscious (fear of abandonment) and interpersonal (relationships) levels. The more levels of power that are involved in protection, the more frequent, intense and enduring are the protective responses, the deeper are the hidden wounds and the greater the need for healing.

Keeping in mind the uniqueness of each person's traumatic experiences and resulting protectors, the following table lists the protectors most commonly employed and the possible healing actions required. I have deliberately refrained from listing the possible wounded areas that the protectors reflect, because the wounds behind any one protector differ greatly from one person to another. Detection of these wounds must be done on an individual basis. If you are unable to trace your wounded parts or have difficulty in healing them, it is advisable to seek therapeutic help.

PROTECTORS	POSSIBLE HEALING ACTIONS
Physical	
Back pain	Try not to turn your back on yourself
Tension headaches	Try to get to and pay attention to the feelings behind the headache
Increased heart rate	Put more heart into caring for self; be aware of and respond to your own needs
Exhaustion	Each day set aside some time, space and energy that is specially for you
Conscious	
Feelings	
Fear	Begin to see your worth as separate from what you do
Depression	Begin to develop a deep love and acceptance of self
Guilt	Provide space, resources and nurturing of self
Loneliness	Embrace yourself and reach out to people who provide safety
Thoughts	
Living in the future	Recognise and use the powers you have in the here and now
Living in the past	Take responsibility for your own healing and growing
Predicting failure/ disasters	Assure yourself of always being there for self in spite of failures
Criticising self/ others	Affirm your own and others' goodness and capability
Worrying what others think	See that your worth is there whether others see it or not
Words	
Blaming self	Know that you have done your best to date
Blaming others	Be responsible for yourself

⟶

Rationalising	Give yourself permission to get things wrong at times and give yourself credit for your ability to learn from mistakes and failures

Actions

Avoidance	Know you have all the resources to take on challenges
Compensation	Work hard on accepting self and becoming independent of others
Withdrawal	Prioritise yourself; discover your goodness and uniqueness
Sulking	Look after the hurt child within you
Aggression	Use your energy to heal your wounded parts
Passivity	Be strongly there for yourself

Preconscious

Feelings

Insecurity	Try to seek out personal and interpersonal safety
Dislike/hate of self	Move towards liking/loving self
Dislike/hate of others	Move towards liking/loving others
Lack of trust in self	Discover your capabilities and trust yourself to take care of self
Lack of trust in others	Create a relationship with self and be independent of others

Attitudes

'Everyone should love me.'	'The most important thing is that I love myself.'
'Nothing should go wrong.'	'Nothing takes away from my lovability and capability.'
'People are only out for themselves.'	'I can be there for myself.'

$\longrightarrow$

'Things will always be the way they are.'	'I have limitless powers to heal and mature.'

Subconscious Fear of abandonment	Unconditionally love yourself

Interpersonal	
Dependence	Depend on self
Approval-seeking	Approve of self
Manipulation	Try to be open and spontaneous
Possessiveness	Become self-possessed
Controlling/ dominating	Be in charge of yourself
Lack of assertiveness	Say 'yes' to self

INTERPERSONAL HEALING

The sources of your blocks to growing are your childhood relationships with parents and other significant figures in your life who, unwittingly, wielded their protective swords and cut into the flesh of your goodness, uniqueness and worth, leaving you vulnerable and insecure. Of course, like you, these individuals who so influenced you were the victims of the protective weapons of others, and it may be that you too in your own life have repeated that cycle by traumatising others with your protectors.

Only in the wake of having created a high degree of both personal and interpersonal safety and some level of personal healing are you ready to go about establishing interpersonal healing. However, if your protectors seriously threaten or are harming others, then those particular protectors need to be tackled immediately.

The process of interpersonal healing is set out below.

STEPS TO INTERPERSONAL HEALING

1. Creation of personal and interpersonal safety (provides a secure basis for the process)

2. Separation from relationships that have in the past threatened or continue to threaten your self-esteem (provides the emotional independence for the process)

3. Development of understanding and compassion for those adults whose protectors caused your wounds (creates a non-judgmental basis for the process)

4. Creation of relationships with others that are of an unconditional, loving, accepting, valuing, encouraging and supportive nature (provides safety for those with whom you interact)

5. Engagement in healing actions directed at the traumatised areas in those individuals who have been cut by your protectors (creates a healing relationship between you and others)

6. Request for healing actions directed at your traumatised areas from those significant persons whose protectors blocked your journey towards self-actualisation

The first step has been covered in Chapter 9. Suffice it to say that when you have dependent relationships on others, you will not be able to heal those relationships until you have some level of both personal and interpersonal safety. The second step is the crucial one. Emotional separation from others (parent, partner, friend, teacher, colleague) does not necessarily mean breaking the relationship with them, but what it does entail is seeing their protective actions as being totally about them and not about you. When such protective actions invade your personal space and your right to determine your own existence, you need to strongly assert your needs and, if your requests are not heeded, you then take the necessary actions to ensure self-determination. Such actions might involve pushing ahead with your own decision (in spite of hostile opposition), not standing around to take verbal or physical abuse, reporting experiences of physical or sexual abuse, pursuing a legal separation from a partner who is abusive. Separation involves becoming emotionally and socially independent of those adults who wounded you and learning to get your recognition from yourself. It is a bonus to be loved and respected by others; it is dangerous to depend on it.

Step three in interpersonal healing has already been discussed. The main point here is the compassionate realisation that those whom you experienced as hurting and humiliating were protectively acting out from their own wounded selves and had no deliberate intention of harming you. They too have been neglected and rejected, and both of you are alike in the sense of the experience of traumatisation and the need for healing.

Step four is required in all relationships so that the unsafe places of homes, marriages, workplaces, and communities can be transformed into havens of safety. People sometimes accuse me of being idealistic when I talk about and encourage the development of unconditional relationships. However, this is an issue that cannot be dismissed as any kind of relationship other than unconditional (conditional or totally neglectful) leads only to fear, insecurity, low self-esteem and dependence within individuals and an uncertain and neurotic society. The person of each human being is sacred and even though protective behaviours that threaten others have to be confronted, this must be done in the context of an enduring, unconditional relationship. Responsibility for threatening actions must be insisted upon but never at the cost of the relationship.

The fifth step – healing actions towards others – raises many regrets for me regarding the hurtful effects of my protective actions on others, particularly my parents, partner, brothers and sister, relatives, friends and colleagues. It is always healing of yourself, and also most times of those you have wounded, to attempt to undo the effects of your protective behaviours on others, particularly those that are of a projective nature – verbal aggression, cynicism, sarcasm, violence, manipulation, criticism and blaming. However, very often protectors of an introjective nature – passivity, avoidance, overprotection, withdrawal, silent hostility, turning a blind eye to abuses – can have an equally devastating effect on emotional, social, sexual, educational and even physical development. Whilst I recognise that I did not deliberately wound people, I must nonetheless take responsibility for the effects of those actions on myself and on others. Apologising is the single most important means of interpersonal healing. A strong indicator of protective relationships is where no one ever apologises. The apology needs to be accompanied by openness regarding the vulnerabilities that led you to act in ways that hurt others.

Sometimes, specific healing actions towards others may be required, actions that are opposite in nature to those that inflicted pain:

PROTECTIVE ACTION	HEALING ACTION
Physical violence	Gentle holding
Verbal aggression	Affirmation
Cynicism, sarcasm	Openness on own vulnerability
Manipulation	Spontaneity
Criticism	Praise for efforts
Blaming	Requesting
Passivity	Genuine care
Avoidance	Honest confrontation
Overprotection	Belief in others' ability

→

Withdrawal	Clear and direct communication
Silent hostility	Honest expression of feelings
Turning a blind eye to abuses	Ensuring caring responses when another is threatened
Dependence	Independence
Destruction of another's property	Restitution

When you begin to show healing actions towards others, they may not be in a safe enough place to be able to trust or receive your caring. In either case persist: do not give to get (this would be conditional), and it may take time for the wounded other person to truly trust your new-found wisdom and loving behaviour.

The last step in the process of interpersonal healing highlights that relationships are a two-way street and that you too have a right to request healing actions directed at your traumatised areas from those who wounded you. You need to take care here; these people may not be able to respond to your requests if they are still locked into a protective cycle of behaviour. Be sure too that, before you make your approach, you feel safe within yourself and have healed, at least to some degree, your traumatised areas. Such a foundation will give you the strength to stay separate, should your request be rebuffed or dismissed or not heard. I recall a client who went to her mother and told her how hurt she had been when she had not been shown love by her as a child, and how she would still treasure receiving affection from her. Unfortunately, her mother had not healed any of her wounded self and replied: 'Well, if I didn't love you back there, then I'm certainly not going to start loving you now.' Fortunately, even though my client felt hurt and disappointed, she did not plummet into despair or rage, but managed to hold on to her regard for herself and compassion for her mother.

Just as the healing actions required of you towards others are often the opposite of those that caused pain, so too the healing actions you may want to request of others will very much depend on the particular protective actions that wounded you. Whatever the outcome of your request, the important thing is that you stay determined to maintain your journey towards self-actualisation.

THERAPEUTIC HEALING

Therapeutic safety is the foundation for therapeutic healing. Indeed, healing has already begun when clients have internalised the therapist's unconditional love and regard for them, allowing them to feel safe to tell their stories, detect their protectors and expose their inner wounds. I believe that, at some level of power, clients know exactly what their problems are and realise that their protectors are vital to their emotional survival. The therapist's main role is to provide the therapeutic safety and ongoing support and encouragement for healing actions. It is not the therapist who is the expert on clients' problems, but the clients. Nevertheless clients need not only the therapist's unconditional acceptance and support, but also the security of knowing that the therapist has expertise in understanding people who have been deeply traumatised and in guiding them towards the necessary healing actions.

It is vital too that therapists recognise the individuality of their clients and the uniqueness of each client's protectors, traumatised parts and their sources. Accordingly, the nature of therapeutic healing needs to differ from client to client. Some clients initially feel safer to work at a purely physical level, others at a behavioural or cognitive level and yet others are ready to work more directly at the subconscious level. What is crucial is that no matter the approach taken or the level of power worked at, therapists need to take their cues from their clients and monitor whether therapeutic safety is being maintained and developed by the particular healing process being pursued. All actions suggested and taken up must occur through mutual decision making. It must be safe for clients to fail, to be indecisive, to be reluctant and even to be hostile to the therapist's healing suggestions. All these responses are protectors; they deserve respect and must be seen as indicators of the necessity for further work on the creation of therapeutic safety.

The therapeutic journey passes a number of essential milestones that are interdependent but do not necessarily follow a sequential path. The primary focus is the healing of the long-protected wounds and the moving on to a greater level of maturity in those traumatised areas. The process is outlined below:

THE THERAPEUTIC JOURNEY

1. Unconditional acceptance and regard for you by the therapist (this creates the therapeutic safety for the adoption of the necessary healing actions)
2. Unconditional acceptance and regard for you by yourself (this creates the personal safety for the practice of healing actions)
3. The creation of some level of interpersonal safety so that there is at least a degree of interpersonal safety in your home, significant relationships, workplace or community for the practice of healing actions and movement to greater maturity in scarred areas
4. Identifying, valuing and respecting of your protectors and the maintenance of these until you feel ready to gradually let go of these creative inventions that have served you so well
5. Use of your protectors as windows into your wounded areas
6. Determination of the specific actions required to heal these areas
7. When healed, the determination of the actions needed to help you mature in your traumatised areas

8. Continual evaluation of the therapeutic process

9. Development of understanding and compassion towards those people who hurt and neglected you

10. Leave-taking of the therapist when you feel ready to continue your life's journey independently (or when not satisfied)

11. Freedom and safety to be able to return to your therapist at any future time should you need further help

---

The duration of the journey, the frequency of therapeutic meetings and the nature of the healing and maturing actions will differ from client to client. The depth and breadth of your protectors and the traumatic experiences you have had will have a huge bearing on the nature and length of your road to recovery and further growing. The ability of the therapist to show unconditional love and the extent of the therapist's own healing journey will also affect your therapeutic journey.

CHAPTER 11

STORIES OF HEALING AND MOVING ON

SAFETY AND THE TELLING OF YOUR STORY

Every person has a story. In my profession as a clinical psychologist it is in the clients' stories that the heart of their conflict is found. Their stories are the maps of all the emotional, social, sexual, educational, political, physical, occupational and spiritual experiences that have brought them to the troubled space they now occupy. It is only when the full story is revealed that true and lasting help can be given.

People will not reveal their stories either to their conscious minds or to others (partners, friends, therapists) until they feel safe. Creating safety is the most important task of the therapist. Safety is brought about by:

- unconditional love and acceptance
- empathy
- absolute genuineness
- non-judgmental approach
- compassion
- active interest in the challenges that face the client
- ability of therapist to communicate verbally and non-verbally all the above.

Partners, friends, teachers, colleagues and workmates can also provide safety for others by engaging in the behaviours described.

There is no more powerful relationship for healthy and mature development than that of the unconditional parent–child relationship. The second most powerful relationship is the couple relationship; partners can provide the intensity of love, regard, interest and celebration of each other that creates the safety so that both can reveal their histories and begin to learn and grow from the unresolved conflicts of past times. A third powerful relationship is that between client and therapist. If parents, partners or therapists are to provide the safety necessary for story-telling, they must themselves have developed personal safety and security. This is why it is so necessary that those who seek to help must have revealed their own stories and, at least, be on the road to healing the hurts experienced. Personal safety and security are not common phenomena and this explains why we live in family, school and social cultures that are largely emotionally unsafe.

Patience is needed in creating safety for another. When you have lived in a world that has let you down frequently, you protectively learn to be distrustful, and a few simple expressions of unconditional regard are not going to lure you out of your defensive space. I have found with clients who have experienced great neglect that it may sometimes take one to two years before a breakthrough comes about. When this happens – when the client has tentatively internalised my love and regard for him – I know that this is the beginning of safety and that the more hidden elements of the client's story may now begin to emerge.

The stories you will read below have been altered in their details in order to protect the confidentiality of my clients, but the essential truth of each story remains. Each story describes how the person, when a child, lost trust in parents, others and the world, and outlines the range of protective reactions at different levels of functioning that were developed in order to reduce further rejection experiences. The healing journeys undertaken are also outlined.

THE STORIES

Each person's story is different and the healing journey undertaken depends on the nature of that story. While recognising the uniqueness of each individual, the stories below cover a range of experiences, with elements of which you may be able to identify. Every client has a different and unique story. That is why every client needs a different therapy.

Lynn's story

Lynn, a thirty-year-old, very attractive, professional woman, presented initially with problems of not being able to cope with the responsibilities of a recent promotion. She was single and had never formed any but the most superficial relationships with men. Neither did she have close relationships with women. Her work dominated her life and her high executive position at such a young age reflected her dedication to work. She did not mix socially with others and had no interests and hobbies outside work. She lived alone in a one-bedroom flat. She travelled home every weekend, even though home was nearly 200 miles away.

The protectors that were revealed during our first meeting were:

Stress and illness
- Abdominal pain
- Nausea
- Tension headaches
- Fatigue
- Trembling hands

$\longrightarrow$

Conscious

Feelings

- ☐ Fear of failure
- ☐ Anxiety about the future
- ☐ Dread of conflict
- ☐ Anxiety in social/work situations
- ☐ Fear of authority figures
- ☐ Performance anxiety

Thoughts

- ☐ Personalisation of what other people said of her (introjection)
- ☐ Living in the future
- ☐ Living in the past
- ☐ Worrying about responsibilities
- ☐ Worrying about how others saw her
- ☐ Rationalisations regarding not forming relationships (for example, 'work takes up all my time' or 'I'm too tired to make the effort to meet people')
- ☐ Poor self-image

Actions

- ☐ Overeffort at pleasing people
- ☐ Perfectionism
- ☐ Avoidance of social risk-taking
- ☐ Overwork
- ☐ Isolation
- ☐ Dependence on parents

Words

- ☐ Non-assertive
- ☐ 'Bottling up' problems

→

Preconscious

Feelings

- Insecurity
- Lack of confidence

Attitudes

- 'I should be perfect.'
- 'I should avoid conflict.'
- 'Nobody would find me interesting.'
- 'Men can't be satisfied.'

Subconscious

- Regression to being a child when threatened
- Fear of abandonment

Underlying these protectors, the *wounds* that became apparent were:

- a feeling of not being loved by either of her parents
- a feeling that she had to prove herself through what she did academically and in her career
- a feeling that her father was a huge source of threat
- a feeling that, no matter what she did, she could not please her mother
- a feeling that she was unlovable, unattractive and incapable
- a feeling that conflict (rows, shouting or silent hostility) was a great source of threat.

The ways her mother and father related to her and to each other were the swords that cut to the quick of her being. Her father was obsessed with his work and had not been involved with Lynn when she was a child. Any contact with him was characterised by irritability, dismissiveness and narcissism. He was unable to show any affection and was not supportive, affirming or encouraging. There were frequent rows between him and her mother that involved a lot of shouting or sulking and withdrawal on his part. Lynn hated these rows and used to run away and hide in her bedroom. Her mother would always be the one who 'brought him around again'. Everything revolved around pacifying her father for 'peace sake'.

Lynn's mother was unable to express affection and had unrealistic expectations of her (and of herself). Lynn used to dread seeing her mother work so hard. She did everything she could to please both her parents – being the 'goodie-good' child and the high performer in school. This cycle of pleasing her parents to the point of gross neglect of herself continued up to the time she came for help. Going home every weekend was her continued attempt to gain the love and regard which she so much craved. This continued dependence on her parents protected her from having to take any risks in forming relationships with others.

Given this traumatic and unloving history, Lynn's range of protectors made great sense. Her unconscious level of power was also active on her behalf, in that, even though she had a major rejection conflict centred on her father (and all other men), she was working in a large organisation of which she was the only female member. This setting provided the ideal situation in which to resolve her feelings of unlovability regarding men.

As for all clients the essential first step in helping Lynn was to create an unconditional loving relationship with her, to show empathy and compassion for her deep hurts and to convey a sense of awe at how she had managed to protect herself from further traumatisation over the years of her life to date. Lynn quickly internalised my regard for and interest in her and this therapeutic safety provided the basis for the following *healing actions*:

- creation of an unconditional love, acceptance, respect and value of self
- development of independence of parents and authority figures so that they were no longer the determinators of her goodness and worth
- separation of her unique identity from work and academic performance so that success and failure no longer were the conditions for her to feel 'good' or 'bad' about herself
- development of conflict-resolution skills and a desensitisation to loud and angry voices, so that she managed to stay in adult possession of herself when she encountered those protective aggressive behaviours in others; commitment to giving 'more voice' to her own feelings and needs
- elevation of her self-esteem so that she had a deep emotional sense of her wonder, beauty and limitless capacity
- adoption (when feeling personally safe) of the challenge of reaching out to others for love, support and friendship, initially with those individuals with whom she felt safest
- development of an understanding of and compassion for her parents (and other significant adults) who were protectively acting out from their own wounded places
- time-management of all her needs so that a healthier and balanced lifestyle began to evolve
- development of a healthy diet, relaxation, regular physical exercise, rest and leisure time.

These healing actions were gradually introduced in Lynn's life. It took over a year of fortnightly visits to establish healing of her traumatised areas and to move on to new challenges that are bringing her further down the road to maturity.

Mark's story

Mark, a twenty-two-year-old single man, was sent to me as 'a last resort'. He had already been seen by a psychiatrist, another clinical psychologist, a counsellor and a herbalist. He presented with delusional behaviours, panic attacks and depression. He had dropped out of third-level college the year before coming to see me and had been largely housebound since then. He dreaded failure and throughout his school years he had experienced panic at examination time. He had learned to 'keep everything to himself'. He suffered from severe eczema, which was a source of considerable embarrassment to him and reinforced his social isolation. He tended to engage in 'comfort eating' and, as a result, was a good deal overweight.

The *creative protectors* he was employing were as follows:

Stress and illness
- Eczema
- Insomnia
- Chronic muscular tension
- Body trembling
- Overweight

Conscious

Feelings
- Feared failure
- Feared punishment

Thoughts
- Worried about examinations
- Had hateful thoughts on his physical appearance
- Worried about parents' reactions to his failure
- Personalised what others said to him

⟶

- ☐ Worried about what people thought about him
- ☐ Believed people saw 'evil' in him

Actions

- ☐ Pleased parents all the time
- ☐ Overate
- ☐ Dropped out of college
- ☐ Avoided social outings
- ☐ Stayed housebound
- ☐ Stayed in bed for long hours each day

Words

- ☐ 'I'm a failure.'
- ☐ 'Things will never change.'
- ☐ 'I've badly let down my parents.'
- ☐ 'People think bad things about me.'
- ☐ 'I'm evil.'
- ☐ 'I'm possessed by an evil force.'

Preconscious

Feelings

- ☐ Chronic insecurity
- ☐ Lack of confidence
- ☐ Feelings of unworthiness

Attitudes

- ☐ 'I should always please my parents.'
- ☐ 'I should be perfectly competent in everything I do.'
- ☐ 'I deserve to be punished when I do wrong.'
- ☐ 'I should not show my feelings of vulnerability to others.'

→

Subconscious

☐ Terror of abandonment
☐ Repression of some violent experiences

Mark's fear of punishment and fear of failure I traced back to the frequent use of violence by his father to exact a perfect performance on assigned responsibilities. Mark recalls being 'hit a lot' by his father. 'Father expected so much of us and I dared not but live up to his expectations.' Neither did he dare show feelings of upset. He cleverly learned 'to keep everything to myself'. Even though his mother was not physically punishing, she also expected a lot and took pride in Mark's academic success. At the age of six years his mother had told him that 'when you are a failure, you are nothing'. His mother's love was extremely conditional on his being 'top of the class'. Otherwise, she showed no spontaneous affection and warmth.

The physical beatings by his father were deep cuts to his self-esteem, and these abandonment experiences were exacerbated by his mother, who did not save him from his father's wrath, and who herself used love as a weapon to whip him into conforming to her unrealistic expectations. During primary and secondary school years he managed, by studying for long hours, to keep up with their expectations. However, owing to this compensatory behaviour, he missed out on his emotional, social and physical development. He formed no friendships, avoided social occasions and played no sports during his school years. It was when he was living away from home, while attending university, that he became immobilised with fear of examination failure and protectively withdrew into deep depression and a delusional world.

Due to being seriously wounded by both his parents, Mark needed to invent very strong protectors. His earlier protectors were compensation (monumental efforts to learn and study), fear of failure and punishment, and suppression of his feelings. He had cleverly worked out, even in his pre-school years, that 'with great effort there can be no failure and with no failure, no punishment and no withdrawal of regard'. He had also astutely assessed that no show of emergency feelings resulted in fewer abandonment experiences. In university he subconsciously dreaded that his strategy of overwork would no longer protect him from failure and so he cleverly resorted to the opposite protector of avoidance – 'dropping out' from college. His depression, eczema, body trembling and muscular tension reinforced his protective avoidance strategy. His protective thoughts, actions and words also strengthened his 'drop-out' status. Clearly, the preconscious protectors (both feelings and attitudes) evolved earlier on continued to drive his conscious and physical protective behaviours. His subconscious terror of abandonment and physical violence was the source of all his presenting protective behaviours, behaviours which were necessary attempts to prevent re-experiencing these traumatic events.

The *wounds* underlying Mark's protectors were:

- rejection by his father
- rejection by his mother
- suppression of both welfare and, particularly, emergency feelings
- a feeling that his worth depended totally on his 'being good, clever and top of his class'
- no sense of his own goodness, worth and capability
- hopelessness about ever gaining unconditional love from his parents
- a feeling that failure was to be avoided at all cost.

With Mark's permission I involved his parents in the therapy so that they could provide the interpersonal safety and support that

Mark needed from them in order to embark on his journey of healing and moving on to richer pastures of living. I hoped too that when Mark's parents revealed their stories this would lead to a realisation on their part that each of them also needed healing. His parents were highly co-operative and, indeed, they too discovered their own protectors, hidden traumas and the actions needed to resolve these hurts. Before working therapeutically with the three of them, I first spent time building a warm, unconditionally loving and humorous relationship with Mark. This relationship made it safer for him to face his parents in the therapeutic sessions with them. What was most clear in helping this family was that each of them had experienced great rejection as children and that each now needed to be redeemed in that wounded area.

The *therapeutic journey* involved the following:

- love and acceptance from me towards each of them
- support and encouragement from me for each of them to demonstrate warmth, affection and caring of each other
- removal of any physical or emotional threat to Mark's self-esteem (great grief was shown by both parents when the effects of their behaviour on Mark were revealed to them)
- demonstration of understanding and compassion towards and by each of them for the protective behaviours that had so blocked the happiness of this family
- development of the self-esteem of each of them through becoming more loving of themselves and independent of each other
- modelling by me of the expression of feelings, encouragement of them to similarly express all their feelings and needs to each other
- realisation that Mark's worth (and that of his parents) needed to be independent of academic and all other performance
- creation of open responses to failure

☐ creation of social opportunities in order to reduce Mark's social isolation.

Owing to the high motivation of Mark's parents, this was largely a joyful journey that maintained its caring momentum up to the point of their leave-taking following about eighteen months of approximately fortnightly contact. Mark returned to university and finished his studies.

Susan's story

When she first came for help, Susan was a single twenty-five-year-old woman, underweight to the point of emaciation. She was a secretary in a small firm where she tended to work long hours so that she got everything right and perfect. Her eating problem had started when she was nine years old and, in spite of several hospitalisations, no change had occurred over the years in her anorexic/bulimic condition. She also displayed irritable bowel syndrome. She lived alone and rarely went to see her parents, who were living not five miles away. She had one brother but had maintained no contact with him. She had no friends and was not interested in forming relationships with men. Her eating problem dominated her life. She would weigh out the exact amount of food she would eat and, if she binged, which she sometimes did, she would vomit up the food. She frequently weighed herself and would panic if she increased her weight (even though she was under six stone). Any extra weight was seen as 'ugly' and 'fat'. She dreaded any situation where she had to eat with others and, if she had to do so, would find an excuse to leave the table and go to the toilet to regurgitate any food taken. She was also a compulsive hand-washer and she kept her flat spotless.

The *protectors* employed regularly by Susan are outlined below:

Stress and illness
- Anorexia
- Bulimia
- Gross underweight
- Irritable bowel syndrome
- Drug dependence (antidepressants and tranquillisers)

Conscious

Feelings

- Guilt
- Depression
- Loneliness
- Hate of self

Thoughts/words

- 'My body is disgusting.'
- 'I must be thin.'
- 'I should not eat sweet foods.'
- 'I don't know how anybody puts up with me.'
- 'People let you down all the time.'
- 'I can never see myself married.'
- 'I must keep myself and everything else spotlessly clean.'
- 'I like to do things perfectly.'
- 'I dread going to work every day.'

Actions

- Worked long hours
- Set unrealistic and perfectionist standards for herself
- Followed strict diet
- Weighed herself frequently

⟶

- Binged occasionally
- Regurgitated food following binge eating
- Attempted at all times to please others
- Avoided social outings
- Kept her flat spotlessly clean
- Engaged in compulsive hand-washing
- Maintained no contact with her parents and brother

Preconscious

Feelings

- Dread of intimacy
- Anger towards her mother and brother
- Overwhelming insecurity
- Hatred of her father
- No feelings of good for herself

Attitudes

- 'I should please others all the time.'
- 'I shouldn't upset others.'
- 'I must never reveal what I feel.'
- 'I should be perfectly competent in everything I do.'

Subconscious

- Repression of sexual abuse experiences
- Terror of being hurt
- Terror of heterosexual relationships
- Fear of emotional abandonment

As for all of us, the sources of Susan's problems lay in the pattern of relationships that operated in her family of origin. She was the first child and her mother did show some care for her until her brother was born two years later. Then her mother transferred all her affection and protection to her son. This cycle of no care and affection for Susan and overprotection of her brother continued up to the time she left home at eighteen years of age. Her father was cold, silent and passive. From the age of five her father sexually abused her and stopped only when she developed her anorexic condition at nine years of age. The anorexia protected her from further sexual abuse and continued to protect her as an adult. Her fear that other men would hurt her as her father had done was a wise protection. Her eating problem was also a metaphor (unconscious power) for the starvation of love she had experienced in her family and continued to experience in her life as an adult. Not being able to stomach food (bulimia) was a further metaphor for her inability to internalise any nurturing for fear it might be taken away again, as it had been when she was two years of age. Her compulsive hand-washing and obsessive cleanliness (which had started at age five years) were unconscious symbols for the need to be rid of her disgust, nausea and abhorrence of her father's sperm and her feelings that her body was 'bad' and 'dirty'. The time and energy demanded by her compulsive actions protected her from getting in touch with the repressed wounds of sexual and emotional abandonment. The severe symptoms of irritable bowel syndrome provided some release of her deeply repressed rage at being so badly abandoned by both her parents; they also reinforced her avoidance of social challenges. Her dependence on medication afforded further numbing of her pain deep within. Indeed, when you examine each of Susan's wisely designed protectors, you can see how each cleverly operated to eliminate any possibility of re-experiencing emotional rejection and sexual abuse. Until these early wounds showed some signs of healing, I was not at all inclined to encourage Susan to let go of her powerful protectors.

Healing and moving on was a long and necessarily slow thera-peutic journey. Susan had lost all trust in men and women due to the neglect perpetrated by both her parents. It took over a year of weekly sessions before a breakthrough occurred when she began to trust my love, kindness and care for her. From this basis of therapeutic safety, I helped her to develop personal safety, through the creation of an enduring and active loving relationship with herself. This involved all the elements of an unconditional parent–child relationship, of which Susan had not even the remotest sense. As caring and nurturing of herself evolved, Susan was ready to move towards healing the wounds caused by the emotional and sexual abuse by her father and the rejection by her mother.

Reclaiming the goodness, beauty and sensuality of her body took considerable time; not surprisingly, since she was coming from a place of viewing her body and her sexuality with loathing and dis-gust. I helped her to see and to begin to hold and nourish the sexually abused child within her and to see that she was the innocent victim of her father's deep emotional and sexual problems. Children who are sexually abused tend to blame themselves as a protection against the possible wrath of the adults who are abusing them. I also helped her to release her repressed rage towards her father but in a way that was not damaging of her or her father. She gradually came to a place where she was able to confront her father, but saw that, even though his abusive behaviour was responsible for her deep emotional wounds, he too was a victim of abuse in his childhood. However, we had to ensure that nobody else was at risk from him. Susan also approached her mother on how hurt she had felt when she had transferred all her affection to her son but, unfortunately, her mother was unable to respond lovingly to Susan's openness. However, at that stage, Susan was quite self-possessed and was able to stay separate from her mother's neutral response. Susan actually felt compassion for her, but realised that her relationships with her father and her mother were not safe places to be. She realised that she needed to find interpersonal safety in other relationships. She now has some good women and men friends but she still feels nervous of committing herself to a permanent heterosexual relationship. However, she has an involvement with a man and it is likely that she will move towards taking the marital risk. She is drug-free and her obsessional-compulsive behaviours are no longer present. Her weight is at a healthy level and she now follows a nourishing diet.

John's story

John, a business man in his mid-thirties, married with two children, was referred by his family doctor for severe headaches and high blood pressure. Medical investigations had found no organic basis for his physical symptoms. In spite of this, John's symptoms had worsened over the period of medical investigation, the reason being that he was extremely worried that he had a brain tumour they were not detecting. John also complained of 'exceptional tiredness' and early morning wakening. Other physical symptoms included nausea and an inability to relax. In spite of the tiredness, he still rose every day (including weekends) at 6.00 a.m. and was at his work by 7.00 a.m. He rarely returned from work before 8.00 or 9.00 p.m. His marriage was under pressure because of his long work hours and he complained that he was missing out on his children's deveopment. The *protective strategies* that he regularly employed were as follows:

Stress and illness
- Severe tension headaches
- High blood pressure

⟶

- ☐ Early morning nausea
- ☐ Chronic tiredness
- ☐ Overweight
- ☐ Insomnia

Conscious
Feelings
- ☐ Performance anxiety
- ☐ Intensity
- ☐ High ambition
- ☐ Loneliness

Thoughts
- ☐ Preoccupied with work responsibilities
- ☐ Living in the future

Actions
- ☐ Overworking
- ☐ Overeating
- ☐ Taking on too many work responsibilities
- ☐ Early morning wakening
- ☐ Avoiding physical/emotional closeness
- ☐ Constant smiling countenance

Words
- ☐ Inability to say 'no'
- ☐ 'Bottled up' feelings
- ☐ Rationalised that work needed all his time

Preconscious
Feelings
- ☐ Dependence on others for approval
- ☐ Insecurity

- Threatened by failure
- Dreaded conflict

Attitudes
- 'Everybody should like me.'
- 'I should be perfectly competent in everything I do.'
- 'Being dependent on others is basic to living.'
- 'People who show vulnerability are weak.'

Subconscious
- Fear of abandonment
- Fear of conflict

The *traumatised areas* giving rise to John's protectors were:

- the experience of not being loved for himself
- the experience that only high academic and work performance gained him praise and some visibility in the family
- the experience that expressing vulnerability gained him only disapproval
- the experience that showing affection merited only ridicule.

John's history is all too typical of many families. His mother was a teacher and highly ambitious for all her children. They had to be 'top of the class' in order to gain her approval. She put considerable strain on herself to be a perfectionist. Nothing was out of place in the home (except, of course, that love was displaced). John's father was a farmer who worked extremely long hours and could not tolerate making mistakes. He was harsh and critical any time John would go out to help on the farm. John learned quickly to conform to his father's ways and to do things perfectly. He also learned to reduce rejecting experiences from his mother by intense study and application to his school work. It was a home in which you dared not be seen to be enjoying yourself or taking your leisure. The emphasis was on work, work, work and on perfectionism. Neither parent was able to show spontaneous affection or warmth. They were blaming, critical, pushing and generally irritable and intolerant of any falling short of the unrealistic standards of behaviour demanded. John's dread of conflict arose from the frequent 'rows' between his parents. He did everything in his power to pacify them.

John's *healing journey* involved the following steps:

- establishment by me of an unconditional relationship with him (this provided the therapeutic safety for him to be vulnerable and gave permission to make mistakes)
- creation of unconditional acceptance of himself by himself (this provided the personal safety for John to separate out from the extreme conditional behaviour of his parents)
- separation of his sense of worth from work and high performance
- development of a balanced lifestyle so that all his personal, interpersonal and spiritual needs were given time and resources
- training in relaxation methods to reduce blood pressure, tension headaches and overeating
- development of independence from his parents' and other people's judgment of his behaviour
- movement towards being able to identify, value, respect and, when necessary, openly express all feelings, particularly those that mirrored vulnerability
- development of acceptance of mistakes and failures as opportunities for learning and not as occasions for criticism.

John made a determined recovery, healing his emotional wounds and moving on to greater maturity in previously protected areas. He also corrected his conditional way of relating to his own children and to his wife, and the resulting happier and closer relationships were a great source of joy and comfort for him.

ENDLESS JOURNEY

I believe the most important journey in life is the journey into oneself. It is the road less travelled due to the lack of safety that surrounds the discovery and celebration of self. Abandonment experiences in childhood, where recognition is gained only through some behavioural performance or where there is no means of being visible, lead us away from any good sense of self. In conditional or neglectful relationships there is no room for your unique and wondrous self to be loved and treasured. It is no surprise then that the path to loving self is rarely trodden. Cutting the ties that bind you to others can come about only through a strong joining with yourself. Paradoxically, the more self-possessed you become, the stronger and more independent becomes your relationship with others. Emotional separation strengthens, whereas dependence weakens relationships.

The journey of healing and moving on does not lead to a life with no emotional or physical pain, but it does lead to safety and maturity so that any pains or conflicts that do arise can be resolved and become opportunities for further growth. Neither does maturity mean never again having to protect yourself. On the contrary, you will use whatever protective responses are needed to combat any threat which may arise to your physical or emotional well-being. However, you will not stay stuck in your protectiveness, but will seek the safety you need in order to learn and move on from the threatening experiences.

The journey into self and out to others and the world is endless. The characteristics of self-actualisation outlined below take many years of healing and maturity to attain, and even then deepening of the experiences could go on forever.

CHARACTERISTICS OF SELF-ACTUALISATION

- Having unconditional acceptance of self and others
- Having compassionate understanding of human behaviour
- Having high degree of independence of others and of behavioural performance
- Openly expressing all feelings
- Being able to be on your own
- Appreciating the limitless power of the human psyche
- Being self-directing and self-responsible
- Focusing on the problem, rather than the person, when there is conflict
- Having a love of life
- Being open to challenges and exploration of your own potential
- Trusting and valuing of self
- Being creative
- Being spiritual
- Being democratic
- Being able to identify with fellow human beings
- Being non-conformist
- Having a caring sense of humour
- Having intimate relationships with a few significant others

BOOKS BY THE CROSSING PRESS

Black Holes and Energy Pirates: How to Recognize and Release Them

By Jesse Reeder

Two phenomena that keep people from reaching their natural creative potential are black holes—unconscious patterns, expectations, and beliefs—and energy pirates—the maneuvering and dodging people do to disguise these patterns and beliefs. Recognizing and understanding human energy fields, and how people are sometimes drained by them, is the key to achieving personal and professional fulfillment. Reeder explains how to overcome these personal barriers to heal and create the life of your dreams.

$14.95 • Paper • ISBN 1-58091-048-3

Overcoming Addiction: A Common Sense Approach

By Michael Hardiman

Psychologist Michael Hardiman addresses addiction with sensitivity and clarity for both the layperson and the recovery professional. He covers addiction's signs and symptoms, explains the psychology behind it, and tells how to stop the cycle for good.

$10.95 • Paper • ISBN 1-58091-013-0

Understanding and Overcoming Depression

By Tony Bates, with foreword by Paul Gilbert

In this book, Tony Bates shares his experiences in treating depression in its many forms and varying degrees, all of them serious for sufferers and their families. He highlights the key strategies that have helped people and outlines a program that both alleviates the shame around depression and provides necessary tools to aid recovery.

$10.95 • Paper • ISBN 1-58091-031-9

To receive a current catalog from The Crossing Press
please call toll-free, 800-777-1048.
Visit our Web site: **www. crossingpress.com**

www.crossingpress.com

BROWSE through the Crossing Press Web site for information on upcoming titles, new releases, and backlist books including brief summaries, excerpts, author information, reviews, and more.

SHOP our store for all of our books and, coming soon, unusual, interesting, and hard-to-find sideline items related to Crossing's best-selling books!

READ informative articles by Crossing Press authors on all of our major topics of interest.

SIGN UP for our e-mail newsletter to receive late-breaking developments and special promotions from The Crossing Press.

WATCH for a new look coming soon to the Crossing Press Web site!